Looking Closely at Learning and Teaching
...a journey of development

Liz Marsden
and
Jenny Woodbridge

with
Mary Jane Drummond
and
Lesley Hill

Early Excellence
Promoting Quality in the Early Years

Early Excellence Ltd
The Old School
New Hey Road
Outlane, Huddersfield
England HD3 3YJ

Tel: 01422 311314
Fax: 01422 311315

web: www.earlyexcellence.com

Published 2005 by Early Excellence Ltd
Copyright © Early Excellence Ltd 2005

A catalogue record of this book is available from the British Library.

ISBN 0-9551041-0-6

Contents

Introduction

Introduction

Welcome to Early Excellence and to our first publication!

At last, we have put pen to paper and are writing about our unique training and resource centre and the work we undertake to promote quality in the early years.

After spending seven years developing Early Excellence within our region, and with the growing recognition our work is receiving nationally, we know that the time is right to document our thinking and capture the essence of our vision.

We are passionate about our work and have a real desire to support practitioners in developing a curriculum that inspires and motivates children and fully engages their powers of thinking and learning. We hope this shines through as we share with you our journey of development.

So what is our book all about?

In part one, we set off on our journey by explaining the core messages that underpin our work at Early Excellence. We present our pedagogical model and examine the key elements in the continuous development of high quality practice.

In part two, we are joined by Lesley Hill, deputy headteacher at Didsbury Road Primary School, Stockport LEA. As one of our practitioner research partners engaged in looking more closely at learning, Lesley takes us through her journey of development, which exemplifies our model of quality in practice.

Part three is by Mary Jane Drummond, who was a lecturer in the Faculty of Education, University of Cambridge, until she retired in September 2004, and is now a regular contributor to Early Excellence activities.

In the two parts of this section she presents first, a commentary on Lesley Hill's work, elaborating on some of the fascinating stories to be heard in this detailed, intimate account of her classroom enquiry. Secondly, she identifies three key features of the Early Excellence model, which contribute, she argues, to both its intellectual and professional strengths and its practical usefulness.

Together we hope not just to engage and inspire you, but also to provide a framework that will challenge your thinking, raising important questions about what matters most for effective learning and teaching.

We hope you enjoy sharing our journey of development!

Liz Marsden and Jenny Woodbridge
Joint Directors of Early Excellence

The Vision of Early Excellence

1

Liz Marsden
and
Jenny Woodbridge

Our journey of development

1998... a moment in time when a germ of an idea, a visit to an old school building and a chance meeting of minds became the impetus for developing the unique centre we have today.

The journey of Early Excellence began in 1998 when we launched our training and consultancy services. Over the next two years, at a time when early years provision was not a national priority, we worked relentlessly across the North West and the Yorkshire and Humberside region to raise the profile of early years education and promote an engaging, meaningful, play-based curriculum.

Our move to larger premises in May 2000, which coincided with the introduction of the foundation stage, strengthened our resolve. We extended our training programme, launched the resource centre and developed an interactive environment to display high-quality provision for children aged three to five.

Now, five years on, we have a well-developed early years centre that is used regularly by practitioners from across our region and beyond. We have good evidence from local authority advisers, headteachers and practitioners that the implementation of the foundation stage has been strengthened by the clarity and consistency of our vision and the quality of our training and resource services.

We now work with a community of educators who...
- have a common approach to planning based on the Early Excellence framework;
- have a deeper understanding of their role in supporting and extending children's thinking;
- have developed well-organised and challenging provision;
- have a firm commitment to, and are developing, the use of the outdoor environment;
- use our language of continuous provision, enhanced provision and adult-directed activities to review and disseminate key elements of their practice.

We are proud of the role we have played and continue to play in our region, and are delighted that our reputation has spread. We are now supporting developments further afield, including the North East, the Midlands, some southern counties and parts of Wales.

Our view of good practice

From the beginning of our journey, including the very first courses we ran, we have shared a consistent view of good practice.

This view is based on our belief that children are powerful and competent learners, who learn best when they are in an environment that connects with their interests, and with adults who value their ideas and engage with their thinking.

In our early days of training for local authorities, when we delivered a significant number of focused and strategically linked courses for early years educators, our vision for good practice ignited a renewed interest in the nature of young children's thinking, and in the importance of play as a key medium for young children's learning.

Since then, the development of our resource centre and interactive environment has given greater visual impact to the ideas at the heart of our vision.

- We promote a curriculum and a pedagogy that give high priority to children's social and emotional well-being, as we know that they learn best when they feel valued, relaxed and secure.

- We stress the importance of understanding children's spontaneous activity, as our experience confirms that when provision connects with children's desires and interests, it makes greater impact on their learning.

- We set high expectations for the quality and organisation of the environment, both indoors and outside, as we believe that a high quality environment inspires creativity, feeds the imagination and promotes many forms of communication and expression.

- We place a strong emphasis on creating a clear framework for children's behaviour, as we understand that learners who 'know how to be' and can act responsibly within the environment, engage in more challenging and creative activities.

- We focus on the role of educators and stress that the responsibility for children's learning lies in their hands: their responsibility to create a rich and stimulating environment, to develop a culture in which children's ideas thrive, and to engage with children in a way that cultivates their ideas and challenges their thinking.

To help us present an overview of these messages, in 2002 we developed a pedagogical model to illustrate the key factors in effective learning.

Our pedagogical model

Our pedagogical model, shown below, presents a view of quality. It illustrates, through three overlapping layers, the key factors in effective learning and teaching.

The simplicity of the model is part of its strength, making it an accessible framework to use in review and evaluation. However, its real strength lies in how it captures the complex relationships between the child, the environment and the adult, highlighting the dynamic processes of everyday life in an early years setting.

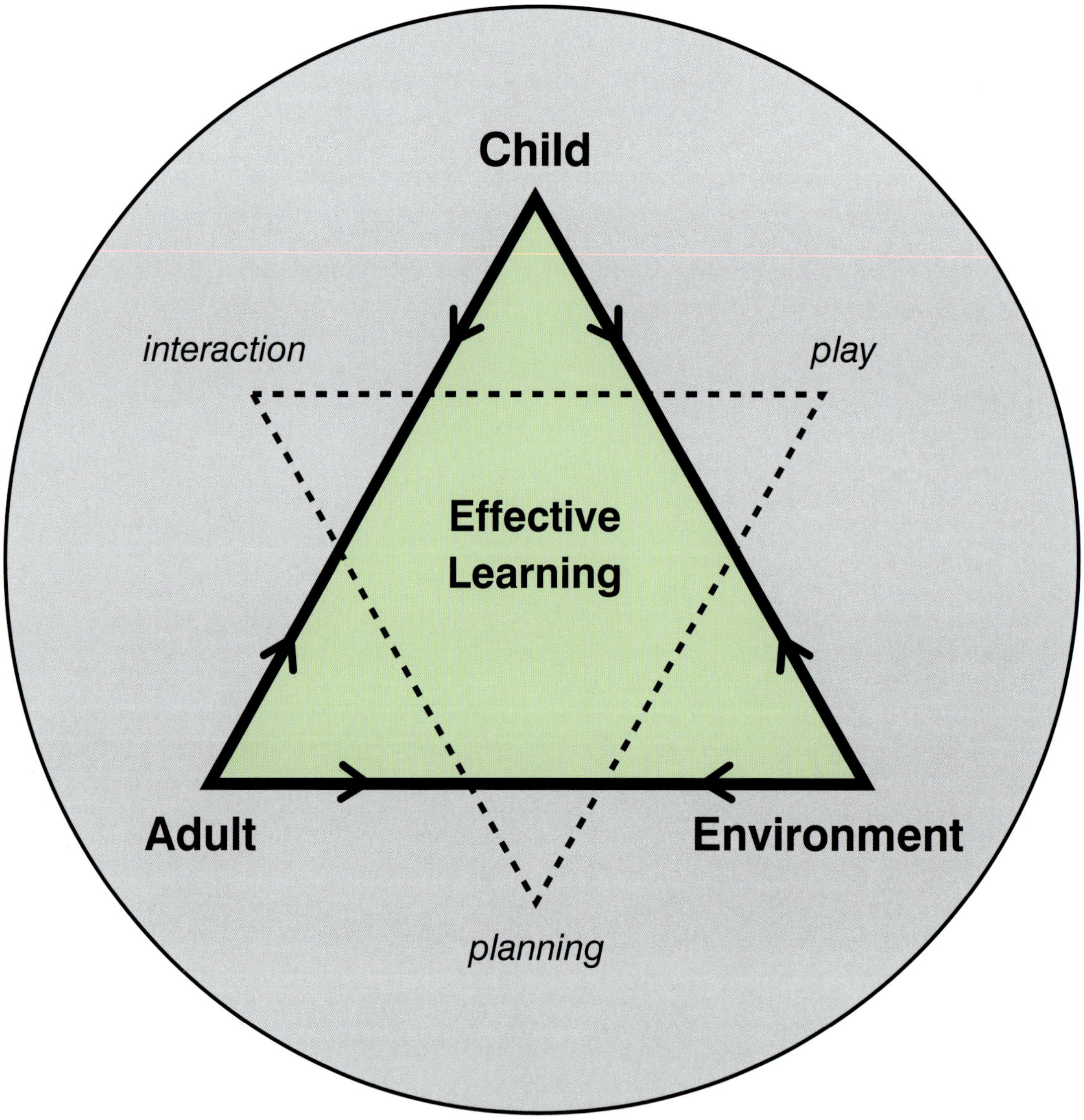

Child

interaction   *play*

Effective Learning

Adult   **Environment**

planning

As you read about the model and begin to understand its significance, you will see how you could use it as a professional development tool, which you can refer to at regular intervals to identify aspects of your practice that are strong and those that need further thought and development.

The key elements in effective learning

The first layer is the triangle shown here in green. It represents the elements that educators need to understand most clearly if they are to develop a foundation stage curriculum that responds to what young learners need.

The following three elements form the underpinning framework for effective learning: responding to children's interests and desires, having an informed view of how best to structure the environment and understanding the role of the educator.

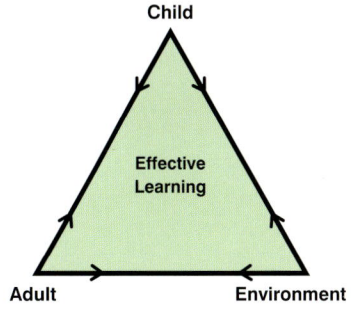

The dynamic processes of effective learning

The second layer is the overlapping triangle shown here as a dotted line. By adding this layer we can represent the processes involved in effective learning and teaching.

- Play - which we see as the dynamic relationship between the child and the environment.

- Planning - which is the way in which educators structure the environment, adapting and enriching their provision in response to children's interests and emerging ideas.

- Interaction - which is the voice of teaching and learning. It is the communication between the adult and the child, in which, through sustained shared dialogue, ideas are exchanged and learning unfolds.

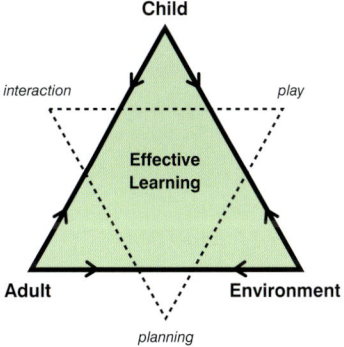

The culture of effective learning

The third layer is the circle that surrounds the two triangles. This represents the culture in which learning and teaching take place, the ethos that pervades what we do and how we do it and defines the quality of our practice.

A supportive culture of warmth and respect fosters children's confidence, motivation, independence and well-being, enabling every child to feel valued and successful.

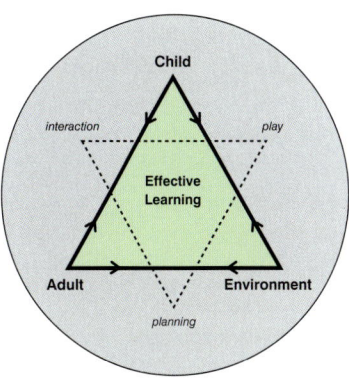

In the following pages we examine the model in more detail. First we take a closer look at the three key elements in effective learning; the child, the environment and the adult. Secondly, we provide an overview of the dynamic processes involved in everyday practice: play, planning and interaction. Thirdly, we explore the importance of the culture in which these processes take place.

The key elements in effective learning

A focus on the child
understanding children's desires and interests

When we introduce our model, we talk about children first and the importance of creating a curriculum that responds to their interests.

In our daily evaluations of practice, what we know about children matters most. Looking closely at children and their play ensures that educators keep in touch with children's lives. Only by deepening their understanding of what motivates children can educators provide experiences that empower them, value their play and take up their ideas.

In this part of our model we invite educators to explore the core of children's lives: their desires and interests in playing, exploring and understanding the world.

In their early years, children have a natural desire to...
- move freely and use all their senses
- talk, listen, ask questions and communicate
- build and construct
- represent and make
- role-play
- story and imagine

These desires are at the heart of children's lives and are central to their learning. They drive the visible behaviours of learning; they are the tools with which children explore and build their understanding of the world.

In their early years, children are interested in...
- themselves and their families
- their immediate environment and everything in it
- their community and the wider world
- the world of fantasy and make believe

These interests lie in the things that children experience most often, the things that they see and feel every day throughout their lives. It is these immediate happenings, a family event, a birthday party, a visit to the shops, a blustery day or a spider's web, a favourite story or TV character, that engage and motivate them.

In working to secure children's well-being we know that capturing what naturally motivates them, their desires and interests, is critical. Responding to children's motivation is highly effective in promoting self-esteem: it is a way of valuing all that is natural to children and giving status to their ideas.

A focus on the environment
developing a carefully planned environment that engages and excites children

In our model, a well-planned, carefully organised indoor and outdoor environment that connects with children's desires and interests, is an essential element of effective learning and teaching.

Creating this environment requires careful consideration and involves the development of two aspects: continuous and enhanced provision. Both these aspects provide structure and enrich the learning opportunities available to children, feed children's self-initiated play and provide the basis for more focused investigations and adult-directed activities.

Developing continuous provision

We use the term continuous provision to describe the resources that are available to children all the time.

In the indoor environment continuous provision is best organised by dividing the available space into small, distinct areas for sand, water, paint, workshop, dough, role play, construction, blocks, books and mark making, maths investigations and music. In each of these areas a carefully selected range of resources is presented in an attractive and accessible way.

In the outdoor environment the space is organised so that children have a range of opportunities for investigative, imaginative and physical play. Key provision includes resources for building and constructing, water investigation, role play, physical activity and games, digging and gardening. In the outside area, a wide range of resources to support these experiences is readily available every day.

In continuous provision, the resources and the way they are organised remain constant throughout the year, offering children a familiar environment in which they can develop sustained play, practise new skills and extend their ideas over time.

Selecting these resources and deciding how best to present them are skilful tasks. To support the development of each area we ask practitioners to think about two questions:

1. What do children spontaneously do in each area of provision?

2. How can educators respond to these spontaneous activities, extending and enriching their
   potential for learning?

> *For example...*
>
> *In the water area we know that one of young children's natural desires is to pour and fill. They do this time and time again as part of their play. By using our curriculum knowledge, we can provide resources that feed these natural desires and promote mathematical and spatial understanding.*
>
> *By selecting graded jugs and funnels and by having two sets of conservation equipment such as beakers and cylinders, we offer greater potential for learning. By presenting these resources individually, in size order, we enable children as part of their play, to think about and use language to describe and compare size, order and capacity.*

Only by taking account of what children naturally want to do and combining this with our curriculum knowledge, can we select rich and relevant resources and organise them in a way that maximises opportunities for learning.

This approach to provision, which gives careful consideration to the range of resources available and the way they are presented, creates a well-structured framework for children's play. It provides a rich context for children's experiences, ensuring that play can be both enjoyable and challenging.

Using enhanced provision

Alongside the development of continuous provision, we promote the use of enhancements as a way of extending and enriching the environment.

An enhancement is a collection of books and resources that connect with children's predictable interests and seasonal themes. They extend learning by offering opportunities for children to develop their ideas and interests. They are also a starting point for new learning, acting as a catalyst for exploring, talking and thinking about new ideas.

In our centre we display a wide range of resources that can be used to enhance the environment.

> *For example... Let's Pretend Garage Mechanic*
>
> *Children love to recreate the experiences around them. In the outdoor environment they often engage in imaginative play with vehicles and role play washing cars, mending them, filling them with petrol, and so on.*
>
> *Our garage collection provides the resources to feed children's interest in vehicle play with, for example, mechanics' jackets, tools and toolboxes, oil cans and traffic cones. It also includes non-fiction books, open and closed signs and number plates to extend children's play and enrich their learning.*

In the indoor environment, enhancements include:

- New books - to support a particular interest, season or festival
- Images and resources - to develop an interactive display around a particular idea or interest
- Interactive trays - using small world or natural materials
- Resource collections - to enrich a provision such as sand in miniature
- Focused collections - to explore a particular concept such as colour or light
- Role play resources - for themed play such as a hospital or shop

In the outdoor environment enhancements include:

- Role play resources - to extend events such as camping, BBQ, picnics
- Investigative resources - such as exploring windy weather, bubbles
- Resource collections - to introduce and develop maths games, pattern making, mark making
- Horticultural collections - to add stimulus to growing and gardening

This approach to enriching the environment is a significant element in effective learning and teaching. Enhancements can be introduced to extend learning within continuous provision, to stimulate children's exploration of new ideas and as the starting point for more adult-directed activities.

For the most effective use of both kinds of provision, children need clear guidance and support in acting responsibly: taking care of the resources, treating them appropriately and co-operating with each other. When adults model how to handle tools and resources, special artefacts and books, children quickly learn to use them with confidence and skill, taking pride in their surroundings.

A focus on the adult
understanding the educator's contribution to children's learning

The most skilful part of our role as educators is the way in which we scaffold children's learning. We provide the bridge between what children already know and understand, and what they will learn next given attentive guidance and support.

It is essential that children are well supported by adults who know how to guide and extend their learning in this way. We emphasise this part of the adult's role, because we know that the quality of their support determines the quality of children's learning.

We encourage educators to recognise two distinct aspects of skilful support.

Responding to the learner

This requires empathy with the learners and a real interest in their thinking. By responding to children, to their ideas, thoughts and feelings, educators promote a strong sense of well-being, creating the safety within which children can push at the boundaries of what they already know and understand.

When educators respond attentively to learning, children are encouraged to:
- ask more questions
- wonder about and puzzle over ideas
- work things out for themselves
- think creatively
- reflect on their ideas

Contributing to the learning

Our commitment to children as strong, powerful and competent learners, full of curiosity to make sense of the world, informs our understanding that children come to learn about their world through discovery and discussion rather than by being told about it. But children also need new information and fresh experiences that promote further learning.

Adults contribute to learning by:
- introducing a new stimulus or a new key word
- giving direct instruction
- demonstrating skills
- modelling language and behaviour
- recording ideas
- documenting and re-proposing ideas

This kind of input is essential. It creates the scaffolding that enables children to reach the next steps in their learning.

The dynamic processes of effective learning and teaching

The second layer of our model is more complex. It represents the on-going processes that are part of effective learning and teaching. It is when educators look more closely at these processes that they can see more clearly how best to act in the interests of children's learning.

The dynamic of play

The first process is play, which we see as the dynamic between the child and the environment.

In high-quality play, children are strongly motivated and deeply absorbed. They actively explore the world, keen to try things out and solve problems. They creatively develop and represent their ideas, showing persistence as they encounter problems and find solutions that satisfy their need to know or do more. They use their imagination to invent new worlds, playing out scenarios and stories that help them make sense of their world, the people they know and their roles and relationships. They express themselves freely, communicate and talk about what they are doing, eager to engage with others who show an interest in their play.

When we observe play that is half-hearted, repetitive or disengaged, we must not doubt children's intrinsic capacity to play whole-heartedly, with intensity and application. We should rather examine our own capacity to organise for and support play in ways that extend children's learning.

By looking closely at children's play, we can learn about the quality of the educators' contribution to play.

The dynamic of planning

The second process is planning, which we see as the dynamic relationship between the adult and the environment. A well-structured environment, which connects with and responds to children's interests, requires careful planning and continual review and development, based on observation and reflection. It cannot simply be set up and left for children to enjoy.

When planning is successful, the environment becomes a totally supportive setting for the many encounters and interactions that take place between children and children and between children and adults. Furthermore, adults can introduce new challenges, fresh ideas and materials, ensuring that this element of the model does not stand still but continues to impact on children's learning.

Looking closely at children's use of the environment will involve staff groups in regular observation and discussion. In their daily/weekly decisions about 'what next', educators can respond to what they have seen of children's ideas and interests. This kind of responsive planning requires staff to discuss children's interactions and their use of resources, recording the significant developments they have noted. They will go on to consider what implications these have, not just for the environment, but for individual children and groups of children, and their developing interests and activities.

It is important to realise that there is more to the educator's task of planning than simply setting up a well-resourced environment. Planning for effective learning entails planning for adult interactions and for children's play, the two other processes represented in our model.

The dynamic of interaction

The third process is interaction, the dynamic relationship between adults and children.

Interaction is an essential part of teaching and learning. But interacting with thinking children is a demanding skill. It requires educators to have a repertoire of strategies for valuing children's ideas and, at the same time, guiding them towards the next steps in their learning.

In the process of quality interaction, children are engaged in sustained dialogue, in exchanges that resemble good conversation, where two or more people share their ideas and feelings. They help each other through their shared experiences, and the give and take of their talk, to understand more.

This kind of interaction, this exchange of ideas, is a serious process and should not be mistaken for a laid back 'make it up as we go along' approach. Educators can skilfully shape their exchanges with children in ways that maximise learning, building a strong reciprocal relationship in which both adult and child have significant parts to play. Through timely suggestions, open-ended questioning and encouraging feedback, educators can foster greater encouragement and interest: these in turn sustain further thought and deeper learning.

Recent research has demonstrated the significance of this kind of adult-child interaction. The important study Researching Effective Pedagogy in the Early Years (REPEY) has convincingly shown that, in the most effective settings, there are significantly more of the interactions described as 'sustained shared thinking' than in less effective settings; the report suggests that these interactions 'may be especially valuable in terms of children's learning' (Siraj-Blatchford et al 2002:10).

By looking closely at the interactions taking place in their settings, educators can evaluate the degree of support and challenge children are offered in their daily activities, and consider the strengths of the strategies they use to sustain children's thinking.

The culture of effective learning

The third layer of our model is all encompassing. It represents the culture within which children's learning flourishes, and the ethos that defines the quality of our practice.

The culture of a foundation stage setting is the outcome of the relationships between adults, children and their families. Where these relationships are warm and respectful, educators create a culture in which everyone thrives, and in which children enjoy the safety and security upon which their learning depends. The qualities of this distinctive culture foster children's confidence, motivation, independence and well-being, enabling every child to feel valued and successful.

By looking closely at the culture in which educators and parents meet and interact, it is possible to review and improve the quality of the conditions that promote effective learning, and enhance ways of meeting the shared responsibilities adults have towards children.

In conclusion

We hope that in these few pages we have presented our model in a way that helps you gain a greater understanding of our thinking and of the factors that contribute to effective learning and teaching.

We know the model offers a useful tool for professional development and hope that it stimulates the necessary process of self-evaluation and improvement at each of the levels represented by its three layers: the key elements in effective learning, the child, adult and environment; the dynamic processes of play, planning and interaction; and the holistic level of culture.

However, knowing that words alone cannot fully illustrate our view of quality, the next part of this book is an authentic example of our model in action: the report of a small-scale classroom enquiry.

As a result of our desire to exemplify our thinking and to illustrate the relationships between the child, the environment and the adult, we organised a practitioner research training programme for a small group of foundation stage educators. It took place in the spring and summer of 2004, and the programme was led by Mary Jane Drummond.

As you read the work of one of our participants, Lesley Hill, deputy headteacher at Didsbury Road Primary School, Stockport, you will see how it relates to our thinking. For the first time we have a significant account of learning and teaching that helps us to evidence, most powerfully, the key elements of our model.

- You will see children's passion for learning shine through and thus gain an insight into how their interests and ideas can be used as a context for extending learning.

- You will see how the continuous environment was developed and how enhanced resources were used to introduce new learning and support children in taking their understanding forward.

- You will see a skilful teacher continually reflect on her role, and, as a result, use thoughtful and supportive teaching strategies that were effective in enriching and challenging children's complex thinking.

Most of all, as you read this wonderful account of four children's learning journeys, you will be captured by the quality of the final and all encompassing part of our model, the culture in which learning and teaching take place.

Lesley understands how to relate to children and develops a positive climate for their growth. She listens to them, enthuses with them, acknowledges their ideas and provides a framework for their interaction and care of each other. They 'know how to be' in their environment.

Lesley accepts that learning takes time and develops routines that give children the space and freedom for thinking to emerge in a relaxed, unhurried manner. She provides the time for children to explore in depth, to be creative as they try out new ideas, to persist as they encounter problems and to think things through as they discover solutions.

Through her interactions, she creates the safety and security that these children need to push at the boundaries of their learning. She nurtures their personal qualities and helps all children, through the responsive style of her teaching, to have confidence in their capacity to learn. You will read about children who feel important, who know that their views matter, and whose ideas are significant in how learning and teaching develop.

It is this positive climate, a culture of warmth and respect, that pervades her work and brings true quality to her children's learning.

We know you will enjoy a captivating read.

'We're all gamesters,' said George

2

Lesley Hill

'When I play a game I like to pretend,' said Katy.

'A good game is if it's like a play – teachers don't need to make them up – we've made the rules and made the game and we are the inventors of games,' Dylan told the group.

'When I play a game I like to pretend they are doing something – they are walking to a snowy park,' said Katy as she moved her penguin along the game board.

'Games make us clever. We listen to each other and when you explain to people – people will get even cleverer. They will know what you know then,' explained George.

'Winning is when you've completed the game. The first one is the first winner and the second one is the second winner and the third one is the third winner and the fourth one is the fourth winner and you never say loser!' Owen told the teacher.

These are just four of the thousands of comments I collected during a five month practitioner research project led by Mary Jane Drummond at Early Excellence.

When I started out I could not have imagined the many different stories that would weave through the games we played. I had started with a games story which I knew would include a maths story and small group story. What I hadn't imagined was the other strong stories that emerged about Dylan, the adults and the other children in the class.

Where to start? As Owen said, 'Start at the beginning and keep going 'til you get to the end. Then you're a winner.'

We shall see.

The beginning

Our reception classes are on a journey. We have already come a long way and we know we still have a long way to go, but we are moving enthusiastically forwards.

With over 450 pupils, Didsbury Road Primary School is one of the largest primary schools in Stockport. Our school reflects our local community. We feel privileged to have large numbers of children with special educational needs as well as children who come from a variety of cultural backgrounds. This helps to make our school a great place to learn and teach.

In our two reception classes we aim to provide a challenging, supportive, well-resourced environment in which children can be creative, resourceful and reflective learners. We want them to become independent learners who are given time and support to investigate and express their ideas and feelings. We want to offer them opportunities to stimulate their knowledge and skills and build on their strengths.

We had already moved away from a curriculum that mainly consisted of unconnected adult-initiated activities provided for reception class children to prepare them for Key Stage 1. We wanted to make a difference to the children's thinking and learning. We wanted to give them opportunities to make connections, to talk about their learning and, most of all, to be 'playful'.

Reflecting on our provision and our practice, we started to ask questions.

Were we providing the right opportunities in all the areas of learning for this to happen? In beginning to set up resourced areas inside and outside, we were thrilled to see how much more the children were interested and excited about their learning. How could we overcome the constraints of the timetable to enable the children to have the extended time necessary to be playful, practise their skills and learn? Feeling brave, we reorganised our timetable and opted out of some 'historic' activities in school that we felt were neither beneficial nor indeed statutory for our children.

We carefully worked our way through the classroom, developing areas with the staff and children. Some were easier to change than others, but that's another story!

The maths area was one of the last to be developed. Why this area last? Did we think the children would only achieve by having a diet of teacher-directed, and sometimes unconnected, activities? Did we really think the children would be stimulated by this diet and be driven to investigate further? Of course not! We were playing safe, just edging slightly out of our 'comfort zone' by taking small but positive steps forward, together. We were trying out our new thinking and planning in the areas we all felt comfortable with. As we developed each area of continuous provision and observed the impact on the children, our confidence grew. We were certainly ready for maths.

Weeks of discussion, planning and organising saw the maths table (where we used to put out equipment that we had chosen) disappear and the maths area evolve. We moved a small shelving unit into the area, purchased a few essential items and we had moved off the 'start' line.

The children helped to organise the area. They were much better than us at choosing storage baskets and boxes to fit different equipment. They weren't so bothered about the aesthetics. The area ended up looking both inviting and exciting and the children named it 'The Maths Shelves'. It was the most popular place to be in Class 1 and if there wasn't a chair free then you just used the floor!

We wanted to link some of the maths equipment to our topic and found we could easily use items that we used in other provision areas, especially the small world toys. It was winter so we used penguins, polar bears, snowmen, trees and winter houses as counters - much more interesting than a coloured plastic disc. We had 30 silver stars and 30 snowflakes (cut from Christmas tree decorations) for counting and sorting and sequencing and...whatever! We had a variety of dice and spinners, sets of numbers to 10, 20 and 30, number lines, some 2D and 3D shapes, whiteboards, writing equipment, number books and *One Snowy Night* by Nick Butterworth, a number story with toys. The shelves were full as was the floor area around them. The children were already used to choosing from various baskets and boxes in the other provision areas and although this area was always busy, it was also always tidy.

What initially amazed the adults was the length of time children spent at the maths shelves and the level of competence at which they worked. Both were greater than previously observed. The children were 'playing' at maths – we had set the area up together, they knew the focus was maths and that was what they were doing. We observed a lot of play in small groups with different kinds of games.

So, on my next visit to Early Excellence I purchased a game board and that's when the fun and games really began!

The game board has a four by ten grid printed onto it with a space for a start and a finish. The children can write on the board with a dry wipe pen which makes the board very adaptable for the children's own games.
It folds in half for easy storage.
It's hard to believe that this very low-cost, low-tech item was the start of so much learning and fun.

Initially adults introduced the game board. They worked with all the children to model games and support them in formulating their own games. The game board was very popular and all the children were both inventive and imaginative - so much more than we were.

During observations at the maths shelves, I noticed that a group of four children frequently chose to play together with the game board. They worked co-operatively and happily talked about their learning. These are the four children who became the focus of this research project: Katy, Dylan, George and Owen. They were all very willing participants, as were their parents, who were consulted about their involvement in this project.

Before we started our sessions I talked to their parents, explained about the research project and gained permission to use their children's work and photographs. Then we were really ready to begin! We played together every Friday morning for the next four months. We had the classroom and all its resources to ourselves for an hour, which certainly was a treat for us all. The four children looked forward to our Friday mornings and when we had to miss one, when the school was closed, they negotiated an alternative day instead. In a preliminary session I used a notebook where I scribbled frantically, trying to capture the children's words. But afterwards I realised how much I had missed.

With their agreement, I started to use a tape recorder and began transcribing the tapes immediately after each session. This gave me access to all their wonderful ideas and thinking. I also tried to capture as many images of the games as I could without disturbing their play. The children are used to being photographed in our classroom, and taking their own photos too, and often asked me to 'take a picture of this, Ms Hill'.

The first thing I discovered was that these five year old children already have a vast knowledge of playing games.

They know that there is a start and there is a finish. They know they throw dice to determine the number of moves; they know they move their counter and that they take turns. As I observed in their very first game in this project, they also transfer their knowledge of the world around them into their games and use language skilfully to talk about their thinking and learning.

I wanted this first game to be my starting point. I wanted the children to devise their own game that I could observe and analyse, to see where to go next. The hardest part for me during the game was keeping quiet. I wanted to answer their questions, help them with their problems, protect them and be their teacher! Did I think they would learn more being directed by me? No, unfortunately, after analysing the transcripts, I found the adult-led games that we played when the game board was first introduced were shorter, less complicated and also less 'playful'. The children didn't have as many opportunities to explore and express their ideas, thoughts and feelings. Sometimes they didn't even have time to think, with adults busily pushing the game on for their own purposes.

During this project I found that I learned so much more about the children's thinking and learning when they took the lead. I used this knowledge to challenge their thinking and encourage them to try new ideas. I also learned a lot about myself as a questioner and listener. Listening to myself on tape was a very traumatic experience!

Every adult working with young children should tape themselves at play with a group of children. Listening to myself on tape has made me think more carefully about what I say, how I respond and also how much I talk. Learning to sit back and listen more carefully to the children, learning to let them take the lead and not always pushing my objective, were lessons quickly learned after listening to several tape-recorded games. I began to see the quality, as well as the quantity, of talking, thinking and learning soaring upwards day after day. It was well worth the embarrassment of listening to those first few tapes!

'Let's play a snowy game penguins and snowy bears,' said George.

So on to the first game: teacher observing and children leading. George had taken the lead and set the scene - a snowy game!

The four children worked together and designed their own game.

Dylan had already told us that 'Polar bears live in the Arctic and penguins in the Antarctic but they can join in together if they like because it's a game!'

Owen had suggested they used two dice 'Like my game at home.'

Dylan said, 'Do numbers on there (pointing to the squares) so the animals can count when they can go up.'

George asked Katy to write 'Start' at the bottom 'because you are good at writing without thinking,' he said.

Katy, who is very confident at reading and writing, wrote 'sart.'

Owen, who is very confident at writing numbers, wrote his numbers in 10s. When he got to the top he had an empty square. He checked by counting up the numbers, '10, 20, 30, 40, 50, 60, 80, 90, 100. No 70!' he noticed and rubbed out the 80, 90, 100 and corrected it.

Now Dylan, who is very confident at talking, was not as confident at writing or recognising numbers past 6 at this time. When he heard Owen say he was writing in 10s he sat back and put his hands on his face!

He quickly sat up, took the pen and announced, 'I'm jumbling mine up.'

'You can't do that Dylan,' said Owen.

Dylan replied, 'I can.'

'Can't,' said Owen.

Katy joined in with 'No Dylan, that's not right.'

To which Dylan replied, 'I can – that's what I'm doing.'

I suggested that Dylan tell the others why he wanted to jumble up his numbers. Already I had broken my silence!

'Thought it would make it more 'funner' for the penguins and bears, they won't know what number they'll go on next. I'm jumbling them up all the way.'

Dylan was very aware that he couldn't always recognise numbers 7, 8, 9 and 10 and frequently came up with amazing strategies to work around this. In the second game he owned up to this, saying he did it to 'make it easier for myself.'

When questioned further he said, 'It was more fun for the animals but it was really easier for me because I get them mixed up anyway.'

Can you imagine how frustrated Dylan would have been on our old maths table? There would be few opportunities for him to explore and express his own ideas and take his learning forward. Would he have the time, or opportunities to work out the strategies which show his fantastic skills as a resilient learner - a learner who persists, remains positive and stays involved in his learning because he feels success and not failure? How many opportunities would he have to show just how clever he is? He is already a winner in this game before it starts, just by taking part in the process of making the game.

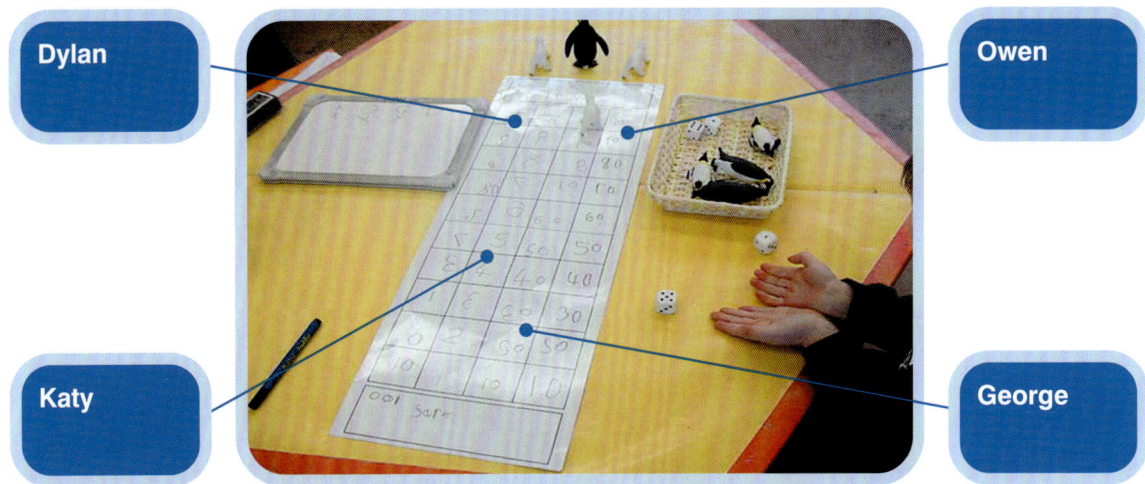

Dylan

Owen

Katy

George

George, who is very confident at thinking, wrote his numbers in 10s next to Owen's. He suggested Owen rewrote his 7 in 70 as it was reversed. Owen rubbed it out and rewrote it just the same, George shook his head and Owen shrugged. Katy wrote her numbers in 1s.

Although we had been working orally in 10s, I had not yet seen any of the children writing numbers in 10s. Dylan's suggestion gave them an opportunity to write for a purpose in their play. The ethos of our classroom provides the security which allows the children to take risks and feel positive about their effort. This came across strongly in all the games we played. The gamesters felt happy to have a go, knowing their efforts would be valued.

Owen suggested they use two dice and explained how to use them, 'Count that one, then that one together.' It was the first time they had used two dice so they practised but soon came to a stop when Dylan got two 6s.

They worked out it was more than the squares on the board.

Owen said, 'If you get to the end you are out.'

To which Dylan replied, 'That's not really fair to be out and you should be a winner.'

George suggested they 'have two winners'.

'One winner when you get over the finish line, one winner for sixes.'

Dylan got a white board and pen from the shelves, gave it to me and said, 'Put all the names on and then put a cross when a 6 comes along.'

I put their initials at the top and gave it back to Dylan to do. The children were working out problems easily without my help!

They were ready for the game.

During the game they helped each other, took turns, talked and listened to each other, added the numbers on the dice, worked out how many more they needed, marked the 6s on the whiteboard and clapped all the winners. More skills than they would have used at one of our teacher-directed maths activities? Certainly - but for me their enthusiasm and focus were the most powerful things I saw. Four children, spending just over half an hour, developing positive attitudes towards themselves as mathematicians!

Dylan finished first. 'You won first Dylan,' George said. They all clapped. 'Katy is second winner,' said George and started the clapping again. Owen was next, then George. At the end Dylan checked the white board and announced, 'I am the game winner and George is the sixes winner. Take a picture of the two winners Ms Hill.' - so I did!

When we first used the game boards we noticed the children clapped when the first child won. The interest in the game waned for each child as they crossed the finish line. We worked hard on this, asking the children about winners and losers. They decided everyone was a winner. It was just first, second, third or fourth winner and no one was ever a loser. The adults actively encouraged this in the children's indoor and outdoor play. As the project went on I was pleased with how this became a culture in our classroom and Katy summed it up perfectly when she said, 'Everyone's a winner in our games.'

Imagine what a difference this principle makes to children and adults. The children had created an ethos in our classroom of 'everyone can do anything!'

Asking the children about what they had learned when the game finished gave me an insight into their thinking and also highlighted issues I could follow up later. The children became more skilful at this as the project progressed and it soon became a well-used question in all our play. Our first efforts were as follows:

Dylan said ━

'I learned numbers are very important things because you find two things and count them. If you had no numbers in the world we wouldn't be able to count and we'd have no money. When Mum and me go to the shop we would get the shopping then the lady would say, 'How many cans do you have?' Mum would say 'What?' She wouldn't even know the word number. Then she'd say how much the shopping was like this 'u, u, u, u,' because there's no numbers. There's no money to pay. Dad would like that!'

George said ━

'We have to make it easy to play, so you win easy.'

Katy said ▬

'I didn't win but it was a good game we made.'

Owen said ▬

'We had to make the game up. We could name this as a game of big numbers and small numbers.'

Dylan added, 'And jumbled numbers.'

Owen said, 'Yes let's call it 'Jumbled Numbers'.'

They all sang, 'Jumbled Numbers, Jumbled Numbers.'

Owen added, 'I go with my Dad when Daniel Furmidge plays football. They make the rules, like you count a goal when it goes in and the Ruler blows the whistle when the football goes off. That's against the law, law or rules - the police say, 'That's against the law' so you don't do it. We had to make it fair. If there wasn't rules it wouldn't be fair.'

A very successful first game with some very powerful thinking and lots of ideas to plan into Game 2.

Adding two numbers together is not a problem for Dylan. He uses his fingers confidently to work out answers! George is just checking he's got it right!

'Stars shine you on your way and snowflakes turn into ice and make you slip back,' said Owen.

After studying the transcript of Game 1, as well as other observations I had collected, I decided I needed to teach the gamesters more about game rules and the aim of a game. I also wanted to introduce moving forwards and backwards in games and, if this was successful, introduce dice with plus and minus signs onto the maths shelves.

I cautiously planned the second game. I hoped I could offer a challenge that would excite and engage the children as well as teaching them new skills. Would I be prepared to let them take the lead and change the game if they wanted? Would I try and steer it back to my objectives? Would I be prepared to abandon my objectives if the children weren't interested? I decided to make the game as 'playful' as I could, as well as being prepared to include their own ideas and connect them into my game where I was able. I was, however, going to stick to my objectives although I had worked out several strategies to get there if I needed them!

I needn't have worried. I set the second game up while the children were outside. They came in very excited to find out what we were going to play.

Reminding them of Owen's comment, 'That's against the law so you don't do it. We had to make it fair. If there wasn't rules it wouldn't be fair,' I asked them what they knew about rules.

'We need rules so we know what the game's like and what you can do in games,' said George.

'And we need to check that all the people are not being naughty like moving too much or going the wrong way,' added Katy.

'Not to cheat. You must not go on anyone else's path,' said Dylan.

'Or you mustn't move yours too many to win,' replied Owen.

I said, 'You're all right. We need rules so we know how to play the game, what we can and can't do in the game.'

Owen added, 'And I know that it's different rules for different games, like my 3D game is different.'

That was just what I wanted to introduce. Owen's short statement had led us straight there!

Throughout the project I was surprised how often the children came up with what I had planned or even went beyond it.

I took them back to the first game again when Owen said after the game had started, 'if you get to the end you are out.'

We discussed the need for everyone to know the rules at the beginning, that lots of games have printed rules you can refer to and that everyone playing the game plays by the same rules.

Through talking, asking questions and challenging each other's answers, they came up with a list of basic rules. They decided that in all the games they played together they would -

- Set up the game board before the game starts.
- Throw a dice to see who starts first.

- Pass the dice round the table (they could choose clockwise or anticlockwise before the game started, but not change direction in the middle of a game).
- Move the correct number of spaces as shown on the dice.
- Not cheat.
- Clap everyone; everyone is a winner - no losers in our games.

These basic rules were used in all their future games and were passed on into the classroom through playing games with other children. Clockwise and anticlockwise became frequently used words in Class 1. Even if they sometimes got them the wrong way round, they knew it meant go round the circle.

On to the aim of the game

In our classroom we explore the learning opportunities with the children, discussing what they can do, what they can learn and reflecting on these opportunities during and after the sessions.

I had never used the word 'aim' so when I asked, 'Aim of the Game, who knows what that means?', I was surprised by the answer, although I could see the connection Dylan had made.
'It's like a target, you know in bows and arrows. You have a target and whoever gets the middle is the winner. In games it's whoever gets to the target wins' (he pointed to the finish).
George decided, 'The aim of the game was getting to the finish by doing what the rules tell you to get there.' We all agreed.

Listening to their responses, I felt like I imagine Vivian Gussin Paley felt when she wrote –

> When they said things that surprised me, exposing ideas I did not imagine they held, my excitement mounted and I could feel myself transcribing their words even as they spoke. I kept the children talking, savouring the uniqueness of responses so singularly different from mine. The rules of teaching had changed: I now wanted to hear the answers I could not myself invent.
>
> (Paley 1986:126)

After Katy said, 'When I play a game I like to pretend they are doing something. They are walking in a snowy park.' Dylan added, 'I know, they are trying to get bows and arrows straight to their hearts.' To which I replied, 'I don't know if these bears and penguins know how to fire bows and arrows.' Later, when I read the transcript of the tape I wish I hadn't. I felt my comment had made Dylan a 'loser.' It was a great idea and my reply let him know I didn't think it was. I suppose at that time, I was happy to let them pretend, but certainly not with bows and arrows!

This conversation reminded me of something else I'd read in Paley's most recent book, in a chapter called 'Young Pretenders': 'We perform a grave error when we remove fantasy play as the foundation of early childhood education.' (Paley 2004:102)

The more I looked at the thinking and learning that took place in the fantasy of games, the more I wanted that 'pretend' in my classroom.

The children are always more interested and participate for longer when we pretend. I found it easier to teach, to pretend with them, and I still got through my learning objectives and more!

Back to the game

George thought it would be good to pretend that 'they could have ice cubes and they could be stepping stones and they go along the stepping stones to get up to their houses.' Owen agreed this was a great idea and suggested they jump over to each ice cube.

All excellent ideas, all imaginative and playful, making this game different from the last.

The gamesters chose a white dice with spots on for the bears and a yellow dice with numbers on for the penguins because as George said, 'The bears are white and the penguins have yellow on them.' The small red dice on the maths shelves was used when we talked about throwing the dice to see who goes first. This very small red dice became the starter dice in every game we played, even in the games outside.

Thinking of introducing moving forward and backwards along the board playfully, I had placed snowflakes and stars inside a set of boxes. I explained to the children that when they had moved their animal they had to choose a magic box. They needed to count the stars or snowflakes to know how many ice cubes to move along. The stars would shine on the way so they could move forward and the snowflakes would block the way so they would move backwards. This was a 'playful' challenge but warmly received by the gamesters who excitedly rattled the boxes and tried to guess what was inside.

Dylan asked,
'Have some of them got snowflakes and stars in?'

They are so much better at making up games! I hadn't thought of that. If I had, would I have dismissed it as too hard? I think so. At the end of the game they requested a mixed box and this is what happened.

'Let's see how it works. If you have five snowflakes and four stars, what would happen?' I said.

Katy replied immediately, 'You would end up there.' (points to one square back)

When asked, she explained, 'You go back 5 and forward 4.'

She moved the penguin back 5 then forward 4 although she hadn't moved it when she worked it out.

'So that it's back 1, because it's 1 less,' she announced.

I said, 'You're right! What about if we have three snowflakes and four stars?'

Dylan jumped in with, 'He will end up there,' (pointing to 1 square forwards). 'I'll show you.'

He lined the snowflakes and stars up in twos. He took away a snowflake and star, then another, then another and was left with one star.

Then added, 'See, 1 forward.'

'Brilliant' I said, 'What about four snowflakes six stars?'

Owen put the stars and snowflakes in a line. 'In pairs,' he said. He moved the pairs into the box saying, 'Count them out.' (He meant as in 'they cancel each other out') 'Count them out, count them out, count them out. Two stars left, count them out. Oh no, they are the same.'

He put them back on the table and added, 'That is 2 up.'

He moved the penguin up the board two ice cubes.

'Here's one for you George, three stars one snowflake.' I said.

George put the snowflake and three stars in a long line. He moved back one square, put the snowflake in the box, then forward each time he put a star in the box.

'He ends up in front!' he declared.

I happily introduced the plus and minus dice in the next game!

The game was a great success, although there were a few problems on the way.

Someone cheated by peeping in a box to make sure it held stars. The others were quick to stop the game, discussing the rules and the law and being fair. At the end of the game when we were discussing what we had learned, that child said, 'I learned not to cheat in games. I'm very lucky anyway 'coz I didn't think I would really win and I did, so I didn't need that cheat anyway. I'll remember next time.'

I found myself referring to Vivian Gussin Paley again. In 'Listening to What the Children Say' she wrote:
> Whenever the discussion touched on fantasy, fairness or friendship ("the 3 F's" I began to call them) participation zoomed upwards. These were urgent questions, and passion made the children eloquent. They reached to the outer limits of their verbal and mental abilities in order to argue, explain, and persuade. No one moved to end the discussion until Justice and Reason prevailed.

(Paley 1986:124)

Through the fantasy play of the game and discussion of the unfairness of cheating, the children exhibited just what Paley had been writing about.

But for me the encouragement and support the 'Gamesters' gave each other were the most exciting things I saw. The hope and anticipation they shared with George as he trailed behind (due not only to lots of snowflakes but also to throwing only ones and twos all through the game) were real and not fantasy.

'Oh no, more snowflakes, poor George,' said Katy.

They all cheered and helped to count when George eventually got some stars!

I was learning so much more about these children being playful in games and was delighted at the end of the game when Dylan said, 'Don't forget a photo of ALL the winners.' Here it is.

As the project progressed, I came to learn just how much these gamesters can do, think, and really know and understand.

Fun seems to be the key to providing opportunities where the children can develop positive attitudes towards maths and see themselves as mathematicians.

These four children have clearly developed positive attitudes towards solving problems; they draw on their already extensive knowledge and skills in their play. They also see themselves as mathematicians; they talk confidently about how they work things out and what they have learned. They are able to make connections and extend their learning through sustained, shared thinking.

Sustained shared thinking is defined by Siraj-Blatchford et al as -

> An episode in which two or more individuals work together in an intellectual way to solve a problem, clarify a concept, evaluate activities, extend a narrative, etc. Both parties must contribute to the thinking and it must develop and extend.

> (Siraj-Blatchford et al 2002:18)

Those words could have been written about these four young children.

As I watched, I saw their thinking in action: solving problems, clarifying ideas, inventing narratives, evaluating their contribution to the game.

The gamesters were clearly displaying their ability to work together in this way. As the games progressed, the children's ability to think and learn and then effectively communicate their findings, kept surprising me. They wanted to play more, I wanted to learn more: it was a most rewarding partnership.

'The aim of the game is snowmen getting to houses through the third dimension,' said Dylan.

I added the plus and minus dice to our collection of dice ready for the third game and the children noticed immediately.

'Look at the new dice,' said Dylan.

'It's adding,' said George.

'Taking away is going backwards in games,' said Owen.

George replied, 'I like the add best; going forward is best.'

Katy said, 'In the other game if you got stars you were allowed to go forwards but if you got snowflakes you had to go backwards.'

Owen's idea was 'that's like the add sign, add it on. I've got an idea, we could use add to go forwards and take away to go backwards.'

They had made the connection. I didn't need my planned introduction.

Then Dylan said, 'What we could do is have two dice (throws +4 –2) so, so, so, you would have 4 then take away 2 mmm you have 4 (uses fingers) take away 2 - that's just 2. Move 2 forward.'

Dylan was pushing the learning a stage further before we had even started: a child who at that time couldn't recognise 7, 8 or 9. During the project I was surprised again and again by the gamesters - how they wanted to learn and develop their knowledge, skills and understanding. Observing them playing games with their friends, I noticed that they never played the same game twice. It always had a new rule, a new aim, used a different dice but always to make the game harder, to make them think and solve problems.

They decided to use only one white dice with plus and minus on this time and used this new dice to rehearse what moves they would make if they were playing a game. Then they started to organise their game.

Dylan said, 'I'll get some counters, snowy people and snowy cottages.'

'Who gets up first to the house goes in, makes a cup of tea and wins,' George suggested.

Owen said, 'It's a snowy day game like it's a snowy day outside.'

Dylan added, 'I've just had an idea. We could move into the third dimension, like in Homer Simpson, where Homer travels to and he has to dodge over the bricks and stuff. We could put these cubes here and you could go up like this and you have to dodge around these (points to the 3D shapes) like this.'

Dylan demonstrated by moving his snowman up to a cube, then across to the next column, up one row, back across to his column and up again.

'These shapes are the third dimension in our game,' said Dylan.

Katy brought over the basket of 3D shapes.

They decided to make the game fair they each needed the same number of 3D shapes. Five was suggested by Dylan, 'I think we should have quite a lot - so we should have five.'

Owen put five shapes on his line. 'That's a lot.'

Katy counted the remaining free squares and said, 'Only five spaces left.'

Katy chose two 3D shapes and arranged them. 'This is my line - I got two shapes.'

They all agree on two and choose and arrange their shapes.

Dylan -   'Mine's a cube and Homer's cone.'

Owen -   'Cylinder and cube for me.'

George -   'Cubes - two of them.'

Katy -   'Cube and a triangle - what do you call it?'

LH (teacher) -   'Triangular prism.'

Katy -   'Triangle prism.'

LH -   'Nearly - it's triangular prism.'

The children discussed where they were putting their shapes.

They all put them on the first two squares.

Katy asked, 'What happens when you get to a shape?'

Dylan answered, 'You go round it like Homer.'

Dylan demonstrated but as all the shapes were together there was no room to move onto the next column.

'Oh dear, how are you going to go round that one?' I asked.

Owen suggested, 'Nodge it like this,' – knocking it sideward onto the next column.

'That's not fair,' said Katy.

Dylan said, 'Just be next to it 'coz it's not your third dimension, it's theirs.'

Owen agreed, 'Yeah, just stay at the edge.'

George spaced his out along his line and the others changed theirs too.

Another game turned into fantasy play, with the counting, the plus and minus signs on the white dice and the 3D shapes all being happily integrated into the play.

'Let's pretend' games provide an exciting and safe context for children to explore and learn. The protection of being someone else allows risk-taking opportunities where the children can investigate and express their ideas and feelings. The open-ended opportunities which fantasy play provides makes this an essential tool for young children's learning. I found the games the children devised provided more possibilities for learning than most of the adult-directed activities on our old maths table. Pretending allows us all to take risks, make mistakes, talk about and discuss ideas and use our skills and strengths, which we don't always get an opportunity to display.

The gamesters used the red starter dice to find out who went first and they were off.
They used the white plus and minus dice correctly and playfully progressed up to the finish line moving around the 3D shapes.

Half way through the game Dylan said, 'I've just noticed that since Katy took that move back, they're all in a diagonal. Take a picture of them in a diagonal Ms Hill. Very good snowmen - smile!'

George finished first and when the dice came round to him again he said, 'I don't need a go because I've finished, I would go off the table if I go again.'
'Not if you get take aways!' replied Dylan.

This comment comes from a young reflective mathematician at play.

Dylan reacted as a mathematician who is able to learn through play, using his skills and knowledge to make connections in his thinking and learning. A mathematician who still can't recognise 7 8 and 9! We learn more about children's knowledge and understanding by observing and listening to them at play than we will ever learn from objective-focussed adult-directed tasks.

Katy was fourth to finish, she kept throwing minus numbers. Her friends were very supportive and cheered her home.

Immediately after the game the children discussed the add and minus signs and how they can be used in sums, 'Like Mrs Furmidge on the easel,' said Katy. During a discussion about '1 more' the teacher had demonstrated how it could be written. Many of the children in the class with older siblings had seen 'sums' before and although the four gamesters are the eldest in their families they all said they had experienced doing sums at home.

The children wrote sums on the whiteboards, telling each other what they were writing. They discussed their answers and corrected and helped each other.

After filling up his board, Dylan said, 'I'm going to give myself a star for doing such good sums.'

'Are you Dylan? And who gives you stars for doing such good sums?' I asked.

'Meself!' he replied.

'Does anyone know what you do to sums when you finish them? When someone looks at children's sums what do they do to them?' I asked.

Katy replied, 'If they're wrong you put a dot there; if they're not wrong you put a tick there.'

'Why do you put a dot there if they're wrong?' I asked.

Katy said, 'Because then they can draw over the dot to put the right answer.'

I asked her who did ticks and dots for her.

'My Mummy,' said Katy.

'My Mum doesn't but I do!' added Dylan.

Katy explained, 'My Mum does it to the children in her school. I see her do it at home in books.'

I said 'Do you know what they sometimes do at school? They give the sums to their friends to mark. You swap with your friend and they mark yours and you mark theirs.' They thought this was a great idea and using a different coloured pen marked each other's sums. They looked carefully at the sums and used their fingers to work out the answers.

They were very complimentary towards each other.

Owen said, 'George is right; congratulations George. It's all right; congratulations.'

George replied, 'You got them all right and the same to you!'

When they had all finished I asked them, 'If you get a big page of sums like this right in school do you know what the teacher would say to you?'

Katy -   'Good sums.'

Dylan -   'She might do a star.'

Owen -   'Say congratulations they are all right and none wrong.'

George -   'Draw a smiley face.'

I said -   'Yes the teacher might. Because you've checked all the answers and they are all right, you can write something on the bottom of your friends' sums that you marked for them. You can be the teacher!'

Katy wrote Gud Suss on Dylan's.

Excitedly George drew a smiley face on Owen's.

Owen wrote Cungrajiachs on George's sums.

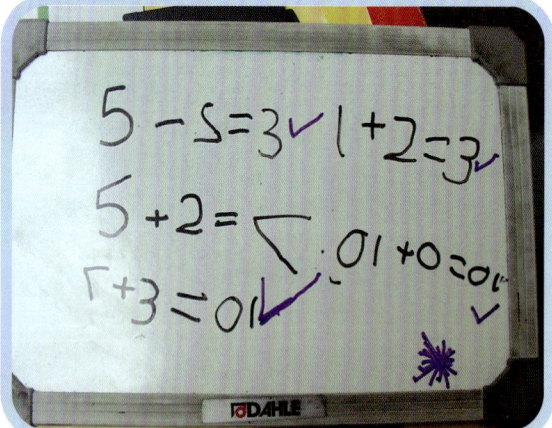

Dylan drew a star on Katy's.

At the end of the third game we talked about what they had learned.

Katy -   'I learned playing a new game if you get a number that says 'add' you go forwards if you don't get an 'add' you go backward, that's a take away.'

Dylan -   'I learned that if you don't try your best you might not win, but it's all about the heart of the game.'

LH -   'What do you mean heart of the game?'

Dylan -   'It's like Yu-Gi-Oh, they are cards, they have a hearts on cards too, playing is good but it doesn't matter if you don't always win first, playing is most important.'

George -   'I've learned that numbers are special to add together to get bigger.'

LH -   'You're right George. If you add two numbers together you get a bigger number, you get more.'

Dylan -   'Except of course with zero.'

LH -   'What happens with zero Dylan?'

Dylan -   'It stays the same; doesn't get bigger.'

At this point he still isn't sure about those 7, 8 and 9s but he certainly knows such a lot about numbers.

Owen -   'I've learned, to do your sums all right your friend gives you smiley faces and ticks and stars.'

Dylan added, 'I know what 100 + 100 is, it's 200. It's just the same as small numbers. You shouldn't be afraid by numbers, like this 500 + 500 is 1000. It's just the same as ordinary numbers. In small numbers its 5 + 5 = 10. 50 + 50 is 100. 500 + 500 is 1000, it's just the same with more zeros on. I used to say 10 hundred - it's just like 10 hundred but its name is one thousand, I can write big numbers too.'

Katy said, 'So can I.'

The children shouted numbers out and Katy wrote them, 40, 70, 55.

Time for lunch. We had been working for 55 minutes and I had learned again not to be surprised by the gamesters knowledge and understanding and also their ability to talk about their learning.

I reflected upon something I'd read in a report about four year olds in school.

> The evidence suggests that in those classrooms where expectations of the children were high, the quality of learning was high. When activities made demands on children's powers to think, to solve problems, to imagine, to create, to build, to express themselves and to organise their work, the children responded actively and with enthusiasm. When the programme required the children to sit and listen for long periods of time, to follow instructions, to produce prescribed outcomes, the children met these expectations, certainly. But opportunities were lost for richer and more rewarding learning.
>
> (Drummond 1995:53)

High expectations of the children by adults have always existed in my classroom. What I was experiencing now was high expectations of adults by the children to facilitate their learning. As we developed more areas we noticed the children became more enthusiastic and much more confident to have a go, ask for things they didn't have and use us to help when they needed us. The quality of learning was high for the children and staff!

Children need to have easy access to a range of resources which inspire and encourage them to initiate their own learning. The gamesters happily used the equipment on the maths shelves as well as confidently using resources from our classroom environment in their play. These confident and independent learners were taking charge of their learning, setting themselves challenges and working out problems. A quick think-back to that old maths table made me feel very proud of us all!

Owen has his own method of adding two large numbers together.
'Put the biggest number in your head and count on from there,' said Owen.

'This game starts in the middle,' said Ms Hill.

Following discussions during the previous games and working with the children in the maths area, I set up the game board before the children came in and wrote 10, 20, 30 and -10, -20, -30 on stickers on a dice. I wanted to introduce several new ideas: a game starting in the middle which allowed them to move backwards on the first throw, as well as the negative and positive numbers that Dylan had suggested with the stars and snowflakes. I also wanted to talk to them about a poster they had designed the day before showing some of the skills they used to help them learn.

I knew they would be excited by the whales and dolphins and hoped that they would connect playfully into my game.

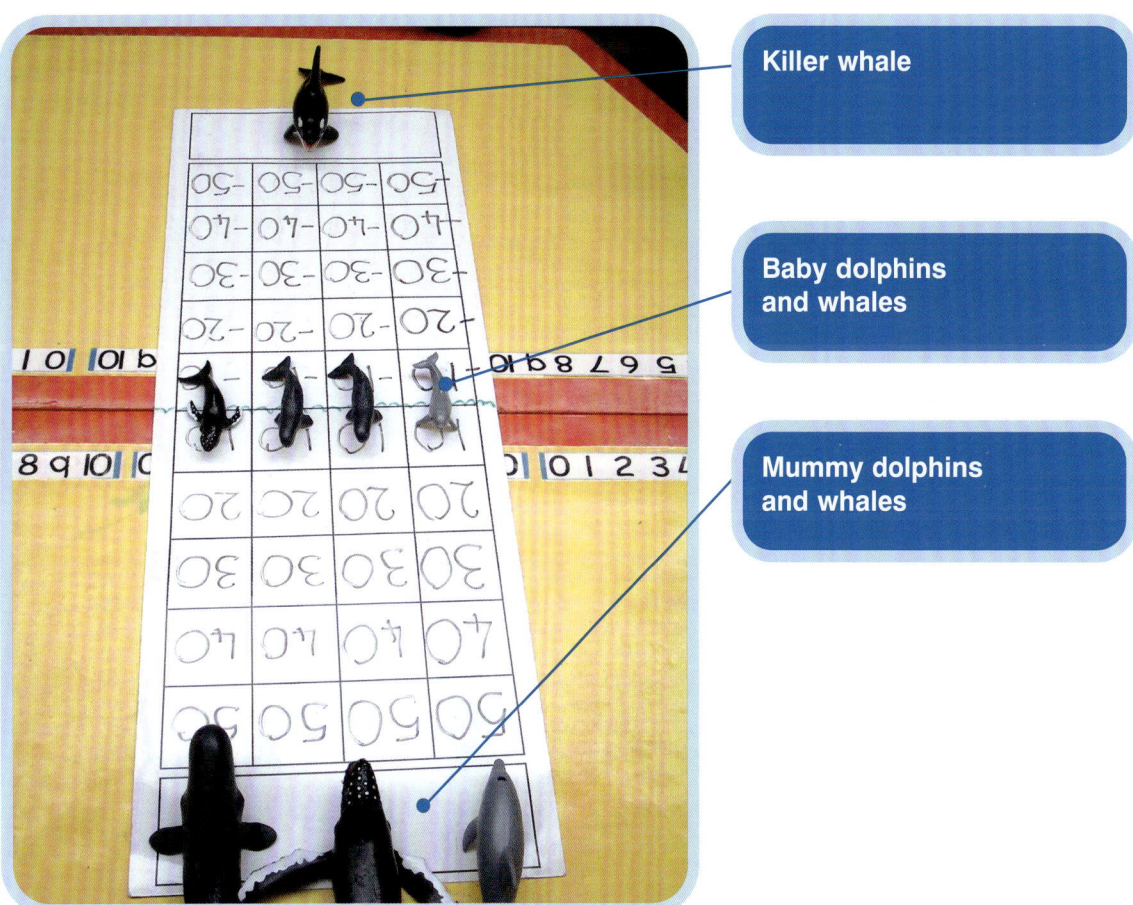

Killer whale

Baby dolphins and whales

Mummy dolphins and whales

The children were very excited and started examining the new creatures and discussing them and the game.

Dylan -   'I saw something unusual as soon as I came over to the game. It wasn't starting with 1 it starts with 10 on evens.'

Owen -   'Not evens Dylan, just counting in 10s.'

Dylan -   'But it's forwards and backwards look.' (points to the minus sign)

Owen -   'Oh yeah, forwards and backwards.'

Katy -   'If you go backwards right down there, the shark will eat them.'

Dylan - 'Me and George can be a team with the same sperm whales. This is a dolphin and that's a hump back whale and that's the killer whale.'

Owen - 'It kills to eat that's why it's called a killer whale.'

Dylan - 'Do you know, the hump back whale can grow to 6 metres?'

George - 'The killer whale grows as big as a double decker bus. It can even eat blue whales which is the biggest in the whole world, but it can't eat sperm whales.'

LH - 'Why not?'

George - 'Don't know.'

LH - 'You'll have to find out and tell me.'

George - 'Yes I'll look on the computer with my dad. The killer whale has the longest teeth in the whole sea.'

Dylan picked up the sperm whale and the killer whale and said, 'It jumps and aims his teeth on their back. I think they like their bones and skin. There are some deadly whales but they don't eat humans; our blood's too warm for them.'

Owen - 'Is their blood cold 'coz they're in the sea?'

Dylan - 'No, ourselves, our blood is warm, we're called warm blooded and sea creatures are called cold blooded. They can drink salt water as well.'

LH - 'What would happen to us if we drank salt water?'

Dylan - 'We would die.'

Owen - 'Is it poisonous?'

Dylan - 'No it's the germs and the chemicals that are in it that make it poisonous.'

Katy - 'Do you have a video of whales Dylan?'

Dylan - 'No - it's all in my book of knowledge. It's got information about all things in the world: no actually not just the world 'coz there is space in it too.'

LH - 'You will have to bring it to show everyone.'

Dylan - 'I'll ask my Dad. He will let me I think.'

LH - 'We will take care of it, tell him!'

What a fantastic example of sustained shared thinking. These four children talking together, sharing information, clarifying facts and questioning each other to find out more.

They spent 12 minutes discussing the creatures, the game board and Dylan's book. We talked about negative and positive numbers, relating it to Dylan's comment about snowflakes and stars. We talked about how, at the beginning of the last two games, they couldn't move backwards when they got a minus number because they were at the beginning. They were very keen to start the game.

Dylan - 'The aim of the game is to get to your Mum. Do not go backwards.'

Owen - 'Or the killer whale will eat them.'

Dylan was first and threw a minus 10.

Dylan - 'See, that's solved that problem. I can go back 10.'

As in every game we played so far, the same person tried to cheat by throwing -20, but only moving 10 back and quickly passing the dice. When challenged by the others the child said, 'Thought you wouldn't notice. Great I'm nearly dead.'

A friend said, 'Still not dead, just on there.'

On the next go the child threw 10 and said, 'It's all over for me, really dead now.' The other three said, 'Ahhh' and all made separate positive comments even though they could see the child was not distressed but just in role as the creature.

In the fantasy of games the children can explore and experiment in all the areas of their learning. They can take risks and try out new strategies happily, knowing that in role it will not be themselves who are challenged but the characters they are playing.

At the end of the game Dylan said, 'Katy got home first to her Mum and Owen got second to his Mum, our Mum's waiting for us still, sniff sniff.'

Katy said, 'It was sad when the Mummy lost her two babies eaten by the killer whale.'

Dylan said, 'I think it was unfair, no swordfish to be the police and stop him eating the babies.'

I wished I had thought of that! In the next session the children designed their own games, and spies and protectors played a big part in George and Dylan's game.

'What did you learn in this game?' I asked.

Dylan began, 'Starting in the middle was easier when you had to go back, there were take away numbers. That's those negative numbers that makes it more funner.'

Then George said, 'All numbers going back from that line are negative numbers and these are the ordinary numbers going up to the Mums. It was a good game and it didn't matter for me to go back with Dylan; he wanted to be with his brother' (points to the baby sperm whale).

Owen - 'I learned that these are negative numbers and these are... oh I forget.'

Dylan and George together - 'Ordinary numbers.'

LH - 'Or positive numbers.'

Owen - 'I thought it was a bit sad for the Mummy that lost her babies. That was sad.'

Katy - 'No one was a winner in this game, the Mummys were winners, well not George and Dylan's, she was sad.'

LH - 'Do you know Katy, I think you are right. That was a very good piece of thinking. Who knows what thinking is?'

Dylan - 'You think about it first, you speak it in your head and then you speak it out from your mouth: that's the important bit.'

Katy - 'If I want to think it's in my brain.'

Owen - 'You have to remember it.'

Dylan - 'In your brain you remember it.'

Katy - 'It gets there from when you listen, tells them what other people have said.'

George - 'And when you talk that's thinking and telling.'

LH - 'You all know so much about thinking. Remember yesterday when we were talking and Dylan said, 'If you don't speak out what you know, you're hiding you're a genius,' and we made a picture of a genius on the computer, well here it is printed out.'

In the classroom we had been talking about the brain and how it helps us to learn.

The whole class were interested and often referred to their thinking brain. They were most taken with the messages sent to the brain from the world around them and how these stimuli made them clever, made them learn more. We designed several posters with the class and put these up in the room. The children often referred to them and told others about them too.

Katy read the whole text. 'I am a genius, I look, I think, I listen, I talk about what I know.'
Owen commented, 'That's a silent 'k' you know. You don't say it.'
Katy said, 'It's a silly word 'coz it should begin with 'n' and just be 'now' (said no).
Oh no, that would be 'now', it should just be 'no' you don't need the k or the w either.'

I wanted to know more from them.

I wanted them to use their growing ability to express their ideas and describe their learning to tell me about the skills they had used in the games. Delving into their learning, questioning and challenging their thinking, I wanted to find out what they knew and be ready to take their learning forward.

Through finding out more, we can offer a range of new challenges that excite and engage the children. By harnessing their natural curiosity, as well as allowing them to share ownership of what is being taught and learned, we can provide those opportunities for sustained and shared thinking we all strive to supply.

I asked - 'If we look at our genius here, let's see if we can think of what skills we used to learn in our game. Look. What did you look at to help you learn?'

Dylan - 'The board.'

Katy - 'The creatures.'

George - 'The dice numbers.'

Owen - 'People who got 'ate'.'

LH - 'What about listening?'

George - 'People learned from listening.'

Owen - 'We listened to Dylan and George about the whales and to you about the numbers.'

Dylan - 'I listened to what they said they learned and I learned that off them too.'

Katy - 'I listened, but they didn't (points at the mummy whales) they were asleep; you can't listen when you are asleep.'

Dylan - 'She won't know anything then.'

George - 'She won't know what to do then.'

LH - 'We've talked about this thinking didn't we, and you are all so good at talking about what you know, I think that makes you all geniuses too!'

Dylan - 'You could make one of those with a picture of us in.' (I draw 4 faces on a piece of paper.)

LH - 'If I put this piece of paper there and pretend it's a photo of you, let's see if it's still right. Help me read it.'

All - 'I am a genius. I look, I think, I listen, I talk about what I know.'

LH - 'Do you think that sounds like you four?'

All - 'Yeah.'

LH - 'So do I. I guess you must all be geniuses too!!'

Powerful thinkers at work indeed.

During the games we played, the children continuously used their new skills and knowledge. It was as if they were adding on another layer to their previous experiences. They were confident to try new ideas and 'layered' these onto their increasing bank of resources too.

By documenting the gamesters learning, giving myself an insight into the 'layering' as it was taking place, I was able to identify what they could almost do and provide opportunities to take their thinking and learning forward.

I was continually revisiting my documentation of the games, trying to reach a more accurate understanding of their learning. The children enjoyed this too. They often asked to see my 'Search for Early Excellence File' as they called it! They loved to look through the pages remembering their games, reflecting on what had happened and what they had learned. They were surprisingly accurate at remembering what each other had said too. 'That was where you said the Mummys were winners. Our Mum wasn't, was she George? Ours was really sad,' Dylan said to Katy, four months after the game!

Documenting the children learning, identifying what they can do, know and understand, as well as what they are interested in and passionate about, is a valuable tool to identify what to do next. I had collected and analysed an enormous amount of evidence so I really should not have been surprised by the amazing first games they designed for themselves, but I was.

I asked the children if they would like to make their own game next time. They were all very excited. The answer was a big YES!!

'We are the inventors of games,' said Dylan.

We sat down together to discuss what we needed to plan and make our game.

They decided:

- They wanted to make two games. George and Dylan working together and Owen and Katy together.
- They would design their games on the white boards. 'It's easy to rub off and draw again,' said Katy.
- The game would then be drawn onto a large piece of white paper using marker pens. 'Can we use those big pens from the easel?' asked Dylan. 'Big pens on the big paper will be quick.'
- They would decide the aim of the game and the rules when they had designed the game. I offered to scribe for them. 'Can you do the rules out like on my 3D game at home?' said Owen. When I questioned him, I understood he meant type out as a games rules leaflet.
- They would choose their counters and dice when they had designed their games. 'We wouldn't know yet about what the game will be about,' said George.

I set the children up on two different tables so they didn't disturb each other and wouldn't be influenced by each other's game. When the game was designed and they started collecting counters they were interested in each other's games and asked each other about them.

George and Dylan

George and Dylan started to talk and draw at the same time. They both agreed on using crabs and fish and a Loch Ness Monster.

Plan

Game

As they were planning and drawing, these were some of their thoughts:

'It's a game for two players,' said Dylan.

'It's a race against fishes, Loch Ness Monsters and crabs,' said Dylan.

'We are going to start in the middle and go up for add ons and down with take aways,' said George.

'Negative numbers you mean,' said Dylan.

'We are having spies to keep an eye on the game. No cheating allowed by the spies,' said Dylan.

'The crabs are the spies,' said George.

'Spies for the audience and there will be cameras too because this game is going to be shown on TV,' said Dylan.

'We'll use the dice with adds and take aways,' said George.

Then Dylan said ━

'Let's use two dice. Watch this Ms Hill, you will be impressed!'

He threw two dice.

George said, 'One step back and four forwards.'

Dylan replied, 'No no no, you don't need to do that, it's 4 take away 1 that's 3. If you get 2 adds you add them together.'

He turned the dice to show + 2 + 2.

'See that's 4 forwards. This will really impress you, watch this.'

He turned the dice to show − 2 − 2.

George said, 'that's 0.'

'No, no, no, it's back 4.'

When I asked him why he said, 'If you get different ones you take away that from that (pointing to the − and + signs) and if you get two the same, you put them together and then go forwards for adds (turns dice to show + 2 + 2) that's 4 forwards, and backwards for 2 take aways (turns dice to show − 1 − 2) that's back 3.'

I was impressed.

Dylan had obviously been thinking about this since the previous games and was able to explain it very confidently to us all. Certainly a young mathematician in action! I thought perhaps Dylan had been talking to his Dad about two minus numbers and they had worked it out together. I asked his Dad the next day and he said, 'No, it was probably just one of his fluky guesses.' I'm not so sure!

Since the first game Dylan has been fascinated by moving backwards and forwards and working out moves using the plus and minus dice. By playing, observing, talking and listening during the games, Dylan has been able to practise this new skill. Again I am surprised by his ability to work out very complicated ideas, but even more amazed at his ability to verbalise them so clearly.

George and Dylan got the paper and markers and carried on talking and adding to and changing the game. The drawn game was different from the plan (see opposite) and they also added more drawings during the game.

> **George and Dylan worked together - planning, designing and making their game.**

Dylan said, 'This is a bit of a Scottish game. Bagpipes are musical instruments from Scotland you know. Och aye the noo. My grandma's from Scotland, you know, don't you Ms Hill. Did you hear her talk like that?'

I said, 'I did hear her lovely Scottish accent, but I didn't hear her say Och aye the noo.'

Dylan said, 'No, she doesn't say that, that's just from Scotland. The Loch Ness Monster's from Scotland and they have fish and crabs; it is a Scottish game.'

Aim of the game

Dylan said, 'The aim's the target' and he added 'a target' at the top in red felt tip.

George added, 'It's a race against the fishes and the Loch Ness Monsters.'

'A race against time too,' said Dylan.

'Yeah a race against time; where's the clock?' asked George.

They got a clock and two timers from the maths drawers.

Dylan announced, 'Let's call this game the 'Race Against Time'.'

George added, 'Yes the 'Race Against Time' and it's against Loch Ness Monsters too.'

Rules

George -   'The baby crabs have to start here and go up to 20, then go back down here to the sand to win; back home!'

Dylan -   'If you get on a fish you go to the side onto these Loch Nessies and next time you go back across.'

George -   'If you cheat you will be spied by the crabs and the octopus. You can't cheat.'

Dylan -   'The bagpipes play a tune when you win. (He hums a tune.) You throw two dice and work out how many to move, backwards or forwards when you know.'

George -   'Highest number starts first, on the red dice.'

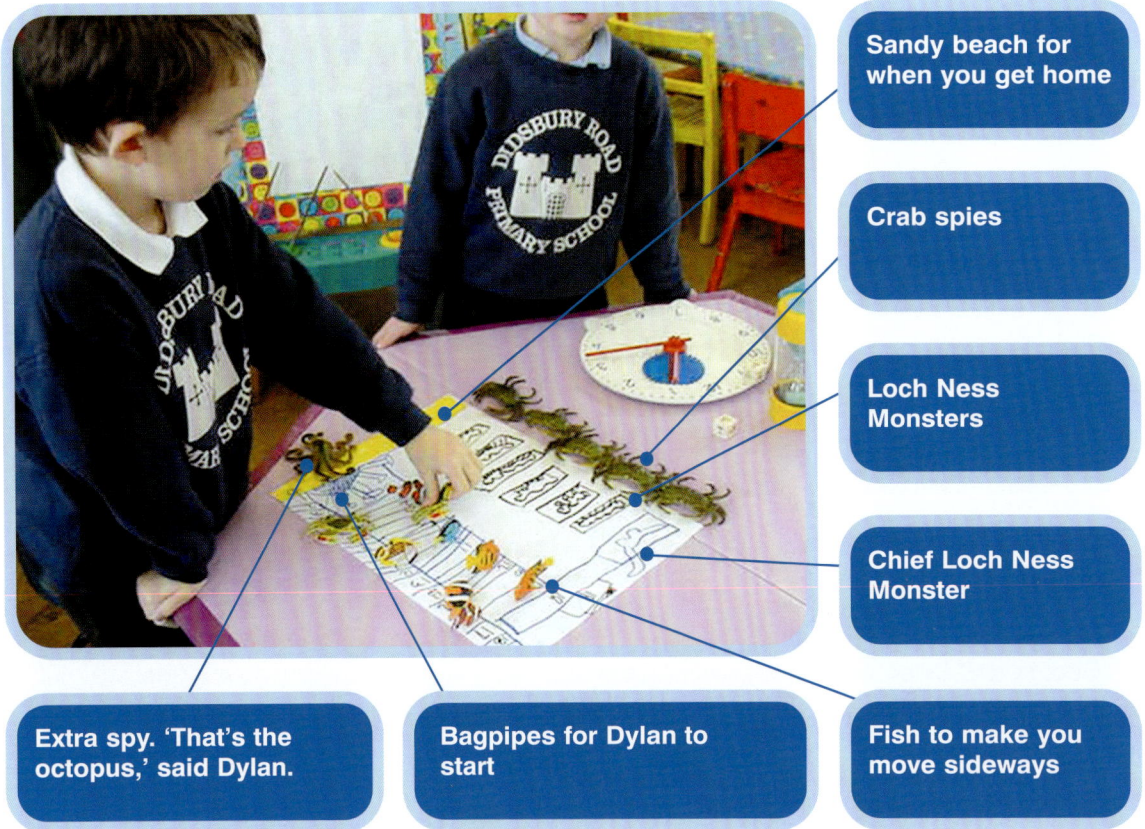

Sandy beach for when you get home

Crab spies

Loch Ness Monsters

Chief Loch Ness Monster

Extra spy. 'That's the octopus,' said Dylan.

Bagpipes for Dylan to start

Fish to make you move sideways

They played the game working out how many to move, moving accurately and following the rules. Dylan drew a pair of red legs with shoes on hanging down from the top of the paper. 'That's the shoes of the man from Scotland,' he said.

George was in charge of the timers and turned them over when necessary. 'That one always finishes first.'

He was using a 30 second and 1 minute timer. I noted this down to follow up later.

George's crab won. He needed 3 to win. When he threw a 6 Dylan told him to start going up the numbers again.

I was just about to intervene when George said, 'No. When you get to the sand you are the winner. It's in the rules.'

Dylan agreed!

After the game I asked them separately 'What did you learn?'

Dylan said —

- Games can teach you other things and numbers.
- Team work and team effort to make games like this and cooperation for me and George together.
- It took ages to build it but we did.
- You have to use your brain, think about other games you play in your brain and you can do your own game, like this one.
- It's clever you know, you get lots of messages sent to your brain and that's how you learn to be a genius.

George said

- Games make you clever 'coz you learn lots about numbers and games.

- I am good at drawing games with Dylan.

- I can write the numbers. I can write numbers to 20. I did it two times, (points to the two tracks) but I can say numbers in 2s to 40. (and he did!)

- You have to think in your brain to tell you what to do.

- In your brain… ummm… your… umm brain collects all the things, you have to be good listeners and lookers, then you think hard to remember it all from there, (points to top of his head).

Katy and Owen

Katy and Owen were sure from the start they didn't want a game that started at the bottom and went up to the top. There was no focus for a theme and no talk of what to use for counters at this stage.

1st plan

2nd plan

Chapter 6

As they were planning and drawing, these were some of their thoughts:

'It needs to be a game of a different shape,' said Owen, 'One that you start in the middle and go out or start out and go in.'

'It's a good game if you want to play it. It doesn't matter about the shape, it needs to have a place to start and place to finish,' said Katy. 'Our game is going to be a different game board to that one' (pointing to the original game board).

They talked about circles and spirals and Katy drew one on the board so Owen could see.

Katy started in the middle and went out in a spiral shape. The lines were very close together.

A wooden maze had recently been installed in our playground. The children were very excited about it and had drawn and painted lots of pictures of it.

'It's a circle maze but numbers couldn't fit in,' said Katy.

'It will be hard to draw squares on a circle game,' said Owen.

Katy agreed. 'Yes, but they have straight lines on a target board for arrows. Put them across like this and it makes the square,' she said.

Owen replied, 'Oh a square that's not a square shape.' He looked at her and shrugged.

Katy said, 'Not a square, a place for the numbers to be in.'

They tried to write the numbers on, but each section was too small.

Katy wrote 'srturt' at the top and 'finiss' at the bottom.

Owen said, 'Make it like our new maze.'

Katy rubbed out the spiral and drew a maze using straight lines on the whiteboard. Starting in the middle and finishing on the outside, she drew lots of lines closely together and started to write the numbers in.

Katy said, 'The numbers are too big.'

I replied, 'They look the right size for your game Katy. Why do you think they are too big?'

Katy thought, 'No not how big (she used hands to show a big size) like this, but its up to 15 now and all that to go.' (pointing at rest of maze)

'Rub it out and do it bigger,' said Owen, 'like this.'

Owen rubbed it out and drew another maze. 'Now do the numbers,' he said.

Katy wrote 'strt' and a zero in the centre and the numbers coming out in numerical order to 20. She wrote 'finish' at the top.

Owen started to put lines across for each section. He stopped at 18.

'We can put lines on it when we do the big one to show where the spaces are,' said Owen.

Katy fetched four rabbits from the small world play. 'These can be the babies and they can get out to find their mummy,' she said.

'It's a maze for rabbits to not be lost in,' said Owen.

Aim of the game

Katy said, 'To find the way out of the maze to 20, then you get out and you are free.'

'Out of the maze to find a big rabbit, it's called 'Get Out of the Maze',' added Owen.

'To get the baby rabbit to his Mummy and give her a kiss like this,' (putting two rabbits' noses together) explained Katy.

Owen said, 'It could be a Mother's Day kiss, a Mother's Day game. It could be called 'Mother's Day for Rabbits.'

Rules

Owen -   'That's the law and definitely no cheats.'

Katy -   'Start on start and finish when you see your Mum waiting.'

Owen -   'No, not see her, when you get to 20.'

Katy -   'Yes, when you get to 20 and give a kiss like this.'

Owen -   'Yes and the more numbers you get that's how many you move. And no going backwards in this game, is there Katy?'

Katy -   'No, only move forwards to get out the maze and kiss the Mummy.'

Owen -   'Throw the dice to see who goes first. Highest number starts.'

Katy -   'That's all the rules.'

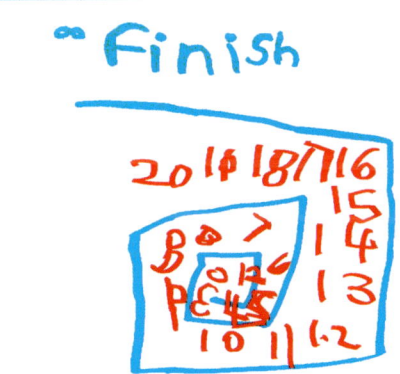

They got the paper and the markers and started to draw the maze.

Katy drew the blue maze and Owen wrote the numbers on in red.

Katy wrote finish at the top. 'There's no room to write start, it's too small,' she said.

They discussed what they could do and decided to start again.

Owen said, 'You do the maze and the lines and I'll write the numbers for you.'

Katy drew the maze in green and blue lines to make the sections.

She wrote 'start' in the centre and 'finish' at the top.

Owen wrote numbers to 39 along the sections, 'That's too many numbers for me to write. The rabbits can just go on the squares to the end,' he said.

They started to play the game and after 6 turns, they had only got to 17 and 18.

'We need more dice and we need to get past 39 and those more. It will be too long to do it,' Katy said.

Owen suggested they used the 10s dice from the last game.

Katy reminded Owen, 'That one goes backwards. We're not going backwards remember.'

Katy asked me for help. 'The dice is too small with those numbers. This game takes too long.'

We discussed using two dice and adding together the numbers but they reminded me that there was only one dice in their rules.

I suggested, 'We could get some stickers and put them on the dice like in the last game but write larger numbers on.'

'Not take aways,' said Owen.

'No, just adds,' I replied.

We put stickers on and got a black felt pen and they discussed numbers and decided to start at 6 and go up to 10.

Katy wrote 6, 7, 8, 9, 10. 'Oh there's one more space left,' she said.

Owen suggested, 'Do another 6 for good luck.'

Katy said, 'Good luck, 6 again.'

They played their game, moving accurately and following the rules. The rabbits stopped to eat grass and play and chat to each other along the way.

'Have a nibble of juicy grass while Owen has his go, baby,' Katy told her rabbit.

Owen spoke to his rabbit then made soft snoring noises. 'Hello baby, you are soon going to see your Mum. Have a little sleep here for a bit,' he said.

Katy's rabbit won and kissed her Mum then watched for Owen's rabbit.

'Look here comes your friend,' she told her rabbit.

Baby rabbits as counters

Start

Dice Katy made

Discarded dice

Numbers for decoration by Owen

Mummy rabbits waiting

'What do you think of your game?' I asked them when they had finished.

Katy said, 'It was too long that game and had too many numbers but the rabbits still liked it.'
Owen agreed, 'Yeah, it was long. It was better though, better than lots of my games at home.'

'I think it's one of the best games I've ever seen!' I told them.

I asked them separately, 'What did you learn?'

Katy said ━

- We can make our own games together if we try.

- We can work hard together and tried our best.

- When you make games, not to put too many on, or it would take too long.

- Do the lines smaller then it only goes to 20.

- You have to think harder to make your own game, your brain knows, um, um, everything. It's big here (touches her head) and remembers everything you've heard before, and touched and looked at as well. Then if you always concentrate it will stay in there and you use it when it's needed.

Owen said ━

- It's hard work to make a game and you have to try and try and try and try to get it right. It was nearly right at the end.

- That I can write up to 39. What is next after that? (I told him to look on the number square).

- Oh yeah, I didn't look there. I should have looked there. It's still a good game without them other numbers isn't it?

- I remembered big numbers from the last game. We had 10, 20, 30. They are big numbers so we can use them again.

- Brains remember what you do and help you think out problems. I was playing with Daniel Furmidge and we had this problem of whose go it is and then our brains both remembered together. 'What did they remember?' I asked. One goes then the other goes and that's fair and we both get goes.

Once again I was amazed. So much to observe and document during the stages of designing, making and playing and so much to analyse to find out what's next after the session.

These resourceful, resilient and reflective learners used their vast knowledge, understanding and skills to work together to design their games. They remained positive throughout the process, persisting with their problems and finding their own solutions. They were able to act upon their past experiences and were prepared to take risks and solve problems. They displayed creativity and inventiveness and used their developing skills to record their work. They were able to access the resources in the classroom independently and had used their knowledge of the resources we have to influence their decisions when making their games. They remained on task, were interested for 55 minutes and were annoyed when the dinnertime bell rang and they hadn't had a chance to play each other's game!

Looking back to the old maths table, I couldn't think of any activities which had produced this amount of excitement and learning. Child-initiated activities, which display children's ability to draw on previous focused sessions, are very motivating for practitioners.

I know I had already become more creative in these focused sessions, being more playful, pretending more and taking the lead from the children. This latest evidence from the gamesters was just what we needed to keep us all moving forward on our journey.

Supportive players, excited by the games, interested in each other's moves, having fun and learning lots too.

The children's enjoyment is written on their faces but they are doing so much more than having fun. They are doing so much learning, of so many different kinds.

Playing each other's games.

Having typed up the rules from the design stage of the game, I read them to the children. I suggested some minor changes to the language to ensure the instructions were clear enough for the game to be used without the designers having to be present to explain.

They talked about the way they wanted it to look.

Dylan suggested, 'A few pictures will cheer it up.'

Owen offered, 'A lot of pictures will cheer it up some more!'

Katy added, 'Put numbers on it so you know which rule is which.'

Dylan said, 'Always put the aim of the game on, this is ours, this target here, remember?'

George suggested, 'Make it big so it won't get lost and reliminate (laminate!) it so it can't get wet.'

We started with George and Dylan's rules.

I typed in the numbers and we searched for pictures.

'Why isn't there a Loch Ness Monster?' asked Dylan.

'It's an American programme. I don't think they must know about the Loch Ness Monsters,' I told him.

'Maybe we should use a Scottish programme then. They know all about them. Loch Ness is in Scotland,' he replied.

We found a dinosaur that was an acceptable shape to them.

George asked, 'What colour is it Dylan?'

Dylan replied, 'Nobody really knows, you see it through the mist.'

George, 'Oh.'

I suggested, 'Maybe we can choose a colour?'

George said, 'Blue is a good one: it's my favourite.'

Dylan agreed, 'Yep, that looks like Nessie now.'

I asked, 'What else do you want on?'

George decided, 'Some crabs and the spy octopus, not the crab spies just the ones to move.'

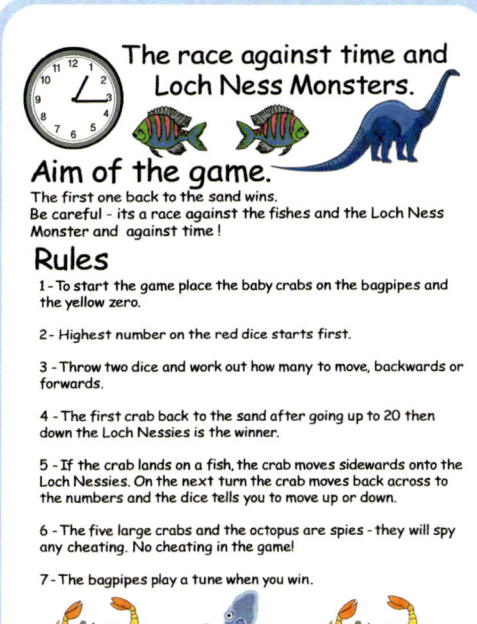

Dylan must have told his Dad about not having a picture of Nessie as he sent in some great pictures on a disc!

We found the pictures and placed them at the bottom. 'So Americans know about crabs and octopus then, just not Nessies!' said Dylan, shaking his head. We put on two fish and decided it was finished.

I read the title, the aim and the rules. 'We need a clock. It's against time remember,' said George. We found some clocks and pasted one on the sheet.

George said, 'That's not the same.' (The hands were on 2 o'clock, not quarter past one as they had used.)

They looked at the photo of their game from last time. We found a clock face and put lines on to make it read quarter past one.

'Great! Print it now,' said Dylan. 'Yeah, print it!' agreed George. We did and then laminated it.

Following on from their comments about the 'Race against Time', and a story I had told them about using my new timer, they asked if they could use it in the game rather than the sand timers.

I asked, 'How long will you set the timer for?'

'Eight minutes. That should be long enough if they go quick,' replied Dylan.

On to Katy and Owen's rules.

'Do you want crabs on yours too?' I asked.

'Noooooooooo,' said Katy, 'that's not right, it's rabbits.'

'Two baby rabbits and two big rabbits,' said Owen.

'Mummy ones you mean,' reminded Katy.

'I thought I could have a Daddy,' said Owen.

'No you can't. It says in the rules 'Mummy rabbits',' Katy told Owen as she pointed to the word 'Mummy'.

'Two baby rabbits and two Mummy rabbits then,' agreed Owen.

We found some Easter rabbits and made two smaller than the others.

Owen asked, 'Shall we turn ours blue like George did?'

Katy thought, 'Yes blue rabbits. That would look great. Have we got a maze picture to put on too?'

We looked but could not find one. I found a border that looked like a maze. It was very wide and covered up some of the writing.

Owen decided, 'That's no good. They can't read the rules with that there.'

Katy agreed. 'No good that maze,' she said.

They decided to choose a different border.

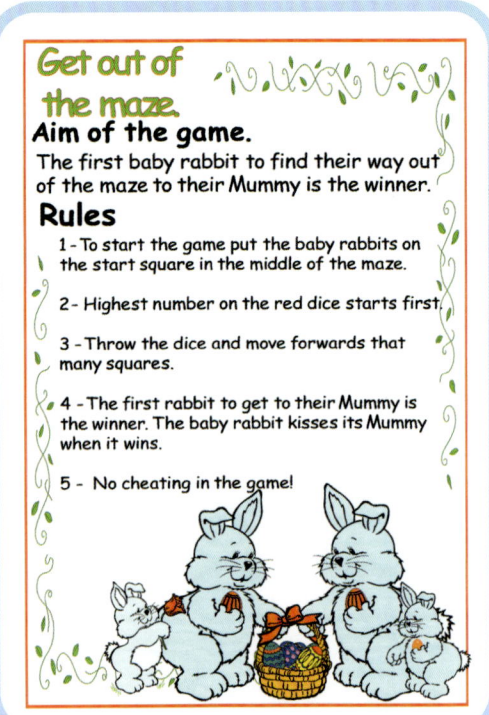

Playing the 'Race Against Time and Loch Ness Monsters' game.

George and Dylan set up the game collecting all their props but had a problem as they hadn't made a record of where the fish were on the board. This was solved by looking at a photo of them playing the game last time.

They explained the rules to Katy and Owen and really enjoyed watching them play their game. Katy was the first winner and as she finished Dylan jumped up and started humming a bagpipe tune. Everyone looked at him. We had forgotten about the bagpipes!

Dylan said, 'That's the bagpipes for the winner, like in the rules there.' As Owen won, Dylan made the bagpipe noises again.

'You won second Owen,' said George.

Owen replied, 'And beat up the time too!'

They all looked at the timer. There were 20 seconds to go. We counted down with the timer and Dylan switched it off.

I asked them what they thought of the game.

Owen said ▬

- Liked all the Nessies trapping you.
- It looks a good game, all those fishes. It's good knocking them down too.
- Two dice are good except when you get two take aways.

Katy said ▬

- Good game. I like it when you move forward and backwards.
- If you don't win first you can win next. This game can be for two winners.
- The crabs and octopus make sure no one cheats. You can't cheat in games.

Dylan said ▬

- The real aim of the game was that target there (pointing to the red target on the board) but everyone missed it, so no one won really!

LH -   'I don't think that's in the rules. It says, 'First one back to the sand wins'.'

Dylan - 'That's right! I give it 10 out of 10, or 100 out of 100.'

LH -   'What does that mean Dylan?'

Dylan - 'If you like it you say 10 out of 10, or 100 out of 100. But if you don't like it you say 0 out of 10.'

LH - 'I suppose if you like it a bit you can say 3 out of 10, or 5 out of 10.'

Dylan - 'No it's just 10 or 0.' (Something for me to pick up on later.)

I said, 'When famous designers design something they say, 'What do you think could make this even better?' What do you think Katy?'

'Make it more exciting with a few more things like crabs to grab you,' she replied.

Owen thought, 'Toy dinosaurs to be the Nessies and the biggest one to be the master.'

'What do you think of it top designers?' I asked Dylan and George. 'Can you think of any way to make it better?'

Dylan said, 'We needed to start in the middle. They both got moved backwards at the start and they couldn't go backwards.' Then he added, 'Two big octopus could have been chasing you. That would make it more of a race.'

George pointed to the feet sticking down and suggested, 'Some little shoes here to make it look real.'
'And a smelly pong for those feet!' said Dylan.

Playing the 'Get out of the Maze' game.

Katy and Owen collected their props and put the rabbits on the board. Then they explained the game.

'You choose a rabbit in the middle and you throw this dice and move,' said Katy.
'Our game is always forwards not backwards. Throw this to see who starts and...where is that one we made, the one with big numbers?'

Katy got the dice and Owen explained, 'We had to make a dice with bigger numbers and before that we had lots of goes and we were still near the beginning. It's better with this one.'

'No cheating in our game as well,' reminded Katy.

They played the game, moving along together. Then George threw four large numbers and went in the lead. Dylan nearly caught him up as the game came to a close.

Dylan threw three 7s in a row and commented, 'Unlucky for some that 7. It's unlucky for me.'

George noticed that he needed 8 to win.

'I'll never get an 8,' he said. (He got a 7.)

'Told you 7 was unlucky for me too,' said Dylan.

George won first and chose the smaller of the two Mummy rabbits.

Dylan said, 'I've got a really fat Mum to get to. I need 8. My Granny says 8 looks like a fat lady.'

'Does she now!' I joked.

Dylan was still finding it hard to recognise 8. These visual images were certainly helping him.

I asked them what they thought of the game.

George said ━

- I liked it. It was a good game. I liked it when I was there and Dylan couldn't catch me up.
- Add a few more numbers to brighten it up right to the end. Me and Dylan liked saying the numbers we landed on.

Katy said, 'We couldn't do it to the end, only to 39 and we did too many squares and Owen didn't know what was the next one to write.'

Dylan said ━

- It was good. There was no numbers there.
- To make it more exciting you could do anything along there that you wanted.
- It should have an audience to watch you get out of the maze.

Owen added, 'The Mums are waiting and they are watching.'

Dylan commented, 'Just two watching? Oh.'

What do you think of it, top designers?
What do you think could make it even better?

'Make it better by not putting so many lines on, Katy,' said Owen.

Dylan said, 'We wouldn't have known how many lines there should be, we didn't see you make the game but you could cut that off there at 37. That would make it shorter.'

'We could put a few more numbers on it, right to the end,' said Katy, 'and get a dice with bigger numbers on from the shops. It was tricky. Ms Hill put stickers on and I did the numbers.'

Owen was looking at the rules for his game and said, 'Look, Ms Hill it says 1, 2, 3, 4, 6. Where is the 5?'
'Well spotted Owen. We will have to change that won't we!'

Dylan and George have collected the equipment many times to play the game with other children. We made a plan to show how it can be set up. The other children used Katy and Owen's game frequently. 'It's a good game to play,' said Daniel.

Dylan asked if he could take the game home to play with his Mum and Dad. He wanted to show them he was a 'top designer.' They decided the order. Dylan and Katy, then George and Owen. We packed up the game, rules and equipment (which we put in a coloured box) in one of our school Book Bags.

Katy said, 'It looks like a game you buy in the shops.'

Dylan said, 'It's better, we made it.'

At the end of the day I didn't need to ask the parents if they would play the games at home. The children, full of excitement, ran out with the bags.

I did ask them if they could write any comments about the game and what the children said.

Dylan's Dad returned -
some comments and a CD with photos of them playing the game at home.

'They're spies, spying on the cheating. If they see any cheating you lose automatically,' said Dylan. Dylan's mum asked him, 'How do you know if the crabs have seen any cheating?'
Dylan said, 'Because we see the cheating and we just pretend the crabs have seen it!'
The game took four and a half minutes to play each time and Dylan always came first!

Katy's Mum wrote -
Katy was really keen to play the game, first with Grandma, then her sister and then her Mum. Grandma thought it was fantastic and was surprised that Katy and Owen had been able to design it themselves. Katy began by reading and explaining the rules and talked about how they came up with the idea by playing in the maze outside.

Throughout the game she was animated and very proud of her achievement. 'I'm really clever aren't I?'

Katy's Mum added -

I've always been impressed with her ability to think around problems but have noticed a difference in the way she articulates and explains her thoughts and ideas recently. For example 'I discovered... because,' 'I imagined this...so' and 'I had a fantastic idea.'

Katy seems to talk a lot about how she learns, her senses and her brain. She counts constantly in different ways and seems to understand addition and subtraction well and makes her own sums up at home. She's enjoying the games and feels special.

George's family enjoyed playing the games too and commented that George had said that the games really help him to concentrate and to count to 20 in 2s!

George's Mum commented -

George is very motivated mathematically. We were amazed, that when in the bath, he spontaneously counts in 2s, 5s and 10s (often to 100) and is counting backwards from 20. He is also recognising numbers to 100 when we play games at home and using mental maths skills e.g. 2 − 1, 3 + 4.

Owen's Mum wrote -

We were not allowed to touch any pieces of the game until Owen had explained the rules. During the game I noticed Owen skipping squares to reach the correct number, eg he was on 28, threw a 3 and went straight to 31. After the game Owen asked for a piece of paper in order to make a chart of how many games each person had won.

She also commented that his personal and social development had improved with playing games and he shares and takes turns with his younger brother now.

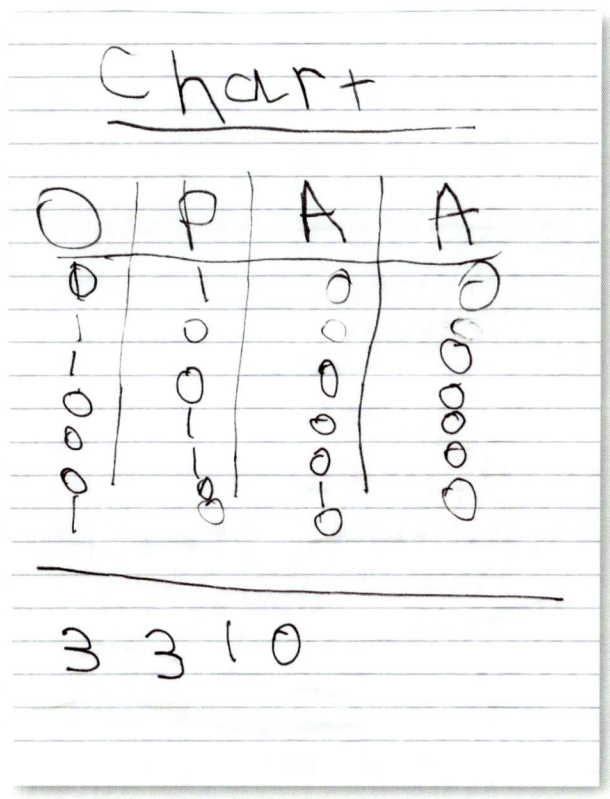

In every reception class, however busy we are, we should make opportunities to share children's learning with their parents.

The information shared is often put into context for us when the parents explain something that has happened out of school. The parents are also vital partners in the assessment process, sharing their experiences and knowledge of their children's learning out of school.

In our school the children are brought into the classroom by their parents or carers each morning throughout their reception year. We have a quiet and safe area for going home too. These are two opportunities where we can have daily contact to share and gather information. We have also developed an area to share information and documentation of the children's learning. The parents (and children) are always proud to see their photos and read about their learning. We also use documentation to support our teaching and the children's learning. It informs and influences our planning. It's a very visual, as well as permanent record, to show just how clever the children are!

Next the children asked if they could design a game outside.

There are many areas where we play in the school grounds but their interest lay in a small area in the playground containing the new maze and traversing wall.
They wanted to involve 'levels' in their game, 'like on a playstation and game boy.'

Dylan said, 'My game has three levels on the houses and then you move up to the climbing wall that's 3, 4, 5 and then to the maze. That's the last level.'

They wanted to design a game by themselves. 'No partners today,' said Katy. But that turned out to be another story all of its own!

Dylan made a plan of the three levels of his game.

Katy wrote down the gamesters scores.

'No cheating in my game,' said George, watching from behind the tree.

'Quiz Time,' announced Owen at the end of his game. 'Close your eyes.'

Playing their own games was both exciting and motivating for the gamesters. They were able to evaluate their games too, talking about what they could change to improve them. Bringing playfulness into maths was a positive step. It had improved the children's skills, knowledge and understanding. It had also provided a playful context to support and develop their learning: a place we could introduce and practise new skills in a fun way. More fuel for our journey - the children were surprising us all the time!

Sharing games in Class 1.

Like all the games the children devised, they were shared with all their friends in the class.

I could see evidence of the skills and knowledge used in these games being used inside and outside, in all the children's play. They would mention the child who had devised the game they had been involved in; 'We counted like that in Jaime's snake game,', 'I learned how to move backwards in Dylan's Fox game,' said Bethany. The gamesters often taught the games we played, or their own version of them, to the other children in the class. We were soon observing these children teaching others. We had a class full of young teachers happily inventing, sharing, correcting, questioning and explaining while they played their games.

Here are just a few examples of the games the gamesters organised in Class 1.

Dylan organised a game with a group of children.

It was a brand new game that he and George made up as the group sat round the table.

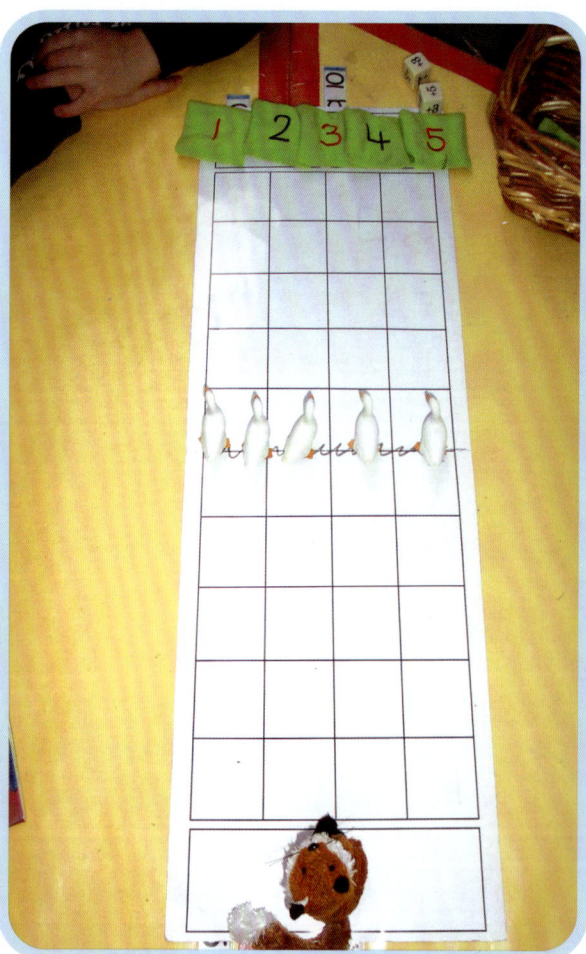

It was based on the number story from the maths shelves called *Nine Ducks Nine.*
He carefully explained the rules and the aim of the game.
'Right, this is the rules. You have to throw a dice to see who starts and the highest number starts. The aim is not to go backwards and to try to get to their houses, sorry, I mean hutches.'

George added, 'And if you get back with the fox then that's the end of you!'

They both rubbed their hands together and laughed.

The group listened excitedly until Dylan started to explain about using the two dice with plus and minus signs on. The interest level plummeted! 'Why don't you use just one dice for this?' I suggested.

Dylan demonstrated how to play to his friends. To make it exciting he used expressive voices for the ducks and fox. He showed them how to move the ducks the correct number and in the correct direction, mostly towards the waiting fox. By being 'playful' he had the group back on board and eager to start.

The children played excitedly and there were lots of shrieks as the ducks moved backwards towards the waiting fox! Jaime ended up in with the fox and when Dylan noticed her sad face he said, 'Don't worry Jaime, you were eaten by the fox this time. You might not next time!'

At the end of the game, I asked him why the other three didn't know how to work out their move using two dice.

He replied, 'They might not know how to do take-aways and adds. They will when they are five. I think Usman's five now. He probably does know really how to do it. It was a good game with one dice anyway.'

Encouraging the children to be imaginative and creative in their games gave them opportunities to explore, experiment, invent and discover. Using their imagination and entering the world of fantasy in their games ensured they were excited and engaged in their learning. Most of all, it gave them confidence in their own ability and made them proud of their achievements. All the class began to develop their skills of imaginative and creative thinking during their play. I observed and documented children displaying skills and knowledge through their maths games I had not previously seen.

Katy especially liked to gather groups of children and organise games for them.

As a confident and independent learner, Katy has great self motivation and perseverance. She is able to express her ideas, take risks, sort out problems and find solutions. She also enjoys the achievement and the positive comments from her friends!

Katy organised a game using ideas from the Homer's 3D game. The children had shells to move around. She carefully explained the rules and checked the children were moving the correct number of squares. She made sure everyone clapped each winner. Her game was so popular that this group played it three consecutive times.

The children were happy to be organised by Katy. She told them whose turn it was next and helped one child count his dice spots and move on the correct number of squares. She spotted someone else moving too many squares and helped him to try again.
She reminded another child, who was new that week to our class, when it was his turn and helped him move the correct number of squares.

I also observed and documented groups of children asking the gamesters to play a game with them. Owen was always the most willing and I noticed he liked to make up new games, usually without using the games board. His games usually had a link to one of the group teaching times that week and were also pitched correctly to the other children's ability. He knew so much about maths but also so much about his friends.

Owen organised a game using the bean bags.

The children had to take turns to pick a bag from the basket and put them in number order in front of them. 'Like this,' Owen said. He had an 8 and picked out a 3. He said, 'Smaller than 8,' and put it on the left hand side of the 8. They continued until all the bags were used. Then Owen said, 'Now you have to say what numbers you've got there and all of us have to check them.'

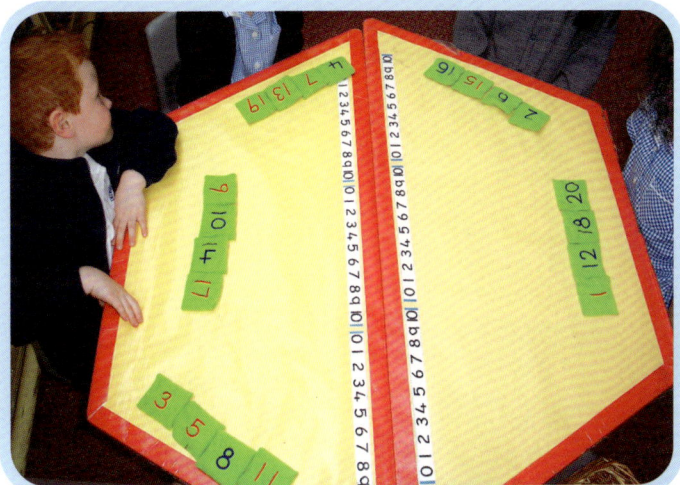

The children talked about odds and evens and how many numbers they had that were bigger than 10, or smaller than 9. One child noticed that if they were given the 4 and 8, they could count in 2s as they had 2 and 6. Another child said they only had 1 even number and 3 odds. So much mathematics going on here!

Owen then organised the group to put the numbers in order. After questioning the children about odd and even numbers he mixed the bags up. 'Just do the evens in order now,' he instructed his friend.

... and he did!

On one occasion Izza came to watch one of Owen's games after it had started. She was sad she couldn't play but stayed to watch the dice game he had organised. Later that day, he made her a card. She came to show me saying, 'Owen has invited me to his next game, look.'

In a culture where innovation, imagination and playfulness are encouraged, the children use all their developing skills in their play.

I observed children using aspects of games played inside in their outdoor play, happily transferring skills into a different aspect of their play. They are able to do this because they feel happy and secure to have a go. They know how to access the resources they need and are given time to plan, try out ideas and play.

The children began to use Owen's method of scoring in their games outside. They also devised other methods of their own. The children were able to explain their methods to others and ask for help from an adult when they needed it.

The children made their own games in the playground with chalk. They often used props for counters, or sometimes themselves.

Bowling

- The children organised this game.
- They used clip boards to keep the score.
- They celebrated each other's strikes.
- They engaged an adult in their play by asking her to 'watch how clever we are at bowling.'
- They took turns at scoring, using Owen's method.
- Two more children asked if they could play for the third game.

As the project progressed, the children began to design and play more games on the whiteboards, on paper and in books.

Their confidence at mark making, as well as their inventiveness, regularly surprised me. Over half of the class were now producing games, quizzes and puzzles on a regular basis. They could work independently, talk about their ideas and also demonstrate their ability to use the knowledge and skills they had been taught. Class 1 had many creative mathematicians at work and I knew that the old maths table could never have produced such exciting work or play.

One example was of Dylan making 'my own 100 square.' George said, 'I'm doing a game all about 20 and the different ways to count to 20.'

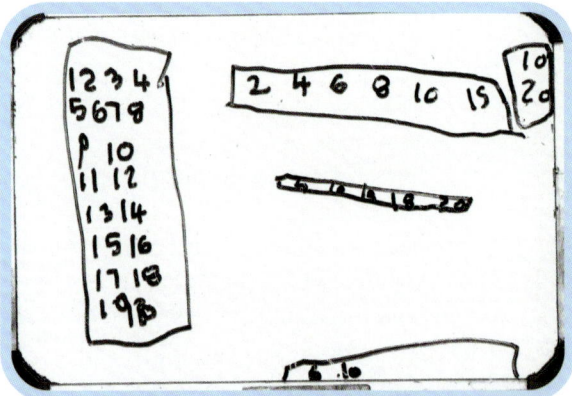

George showed his fantastic numbers to the group, Barbarella chose the same equipment later in the day and although she could not see George's, she produced her own game and played it with her friends. The children knew I could use the photocopier to reproduce their games and liked the freedom to rub out and redesign.

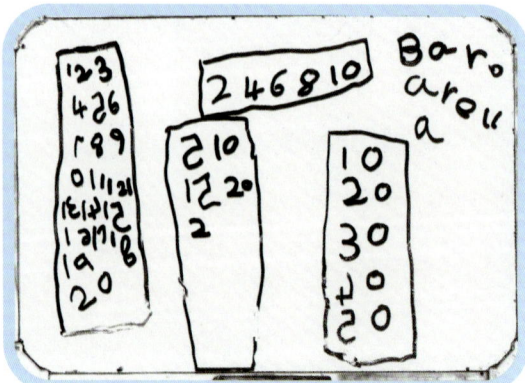

The children were beginning to provide their own opportunities to develop and practise skills. Thinking back to the beginning of the project, I don't think I could ever have imagined seeing George and Dylan test each other!

When I spotted them in the maths area they were playing a game, 'a sum quiz', said George. 'We are testing each other,' said Dylan.

Dylan had a red pen and George had a black pen. George wrote a sum for Dylan. Dylan wrote the answer and then wrote a sum for George. They were on the fourth sum when I got there.

Dylan said, 'This is a tricky one for you George 2-1=?' George said, 'Easy, that's 1.'

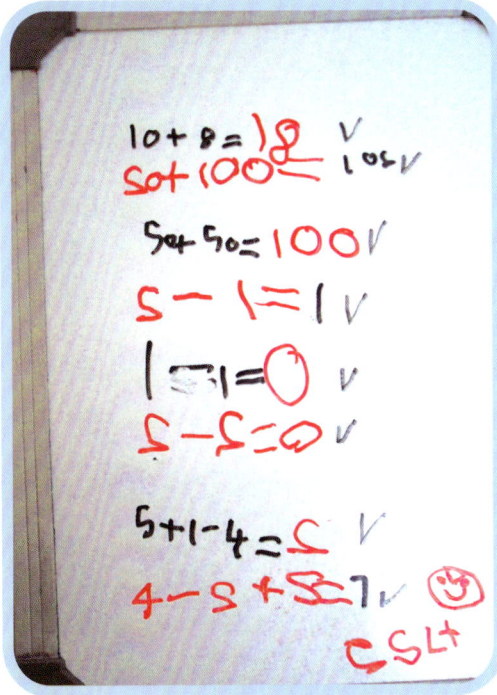

George wrote 1 = 1 = and said, 'That's even more tricky for you.'

Dylan noticed, 'That's a make sign' (pointing to where a minus sign should be).

George replied, 'Oh yeah', then changed it.

'1 take away 1 that's zero,' said Dylan. He then wrote 2 − 2 = for George.

George said, 'You can do the zero answer for me. I know that one.' Dylan wrote an 0 for him.

George took the board and wrote 5 + 1 − 4 =

Dylan said, '5 + 1 − 4 that's 6, then get 6 and take away 4.' Dylan put up six fingers, then put down four and wrote 2 as the answer.

Dylan wrote 4 − 2 + 5 =

George looked at the sum. 'That's 2,' he said. He put up five fingers on the other hand.

Before George had a chance to say anything Dylan said, 'Add those and those for the answer.'

George said, 'I'm doing it now, wait.' George counted his fingers and wrote 7.

Dylan congratulated him. 'Great, George,' he said.

'I will do the ticks for the sums,' announced George.

George checked all the sums while Dylan sat and watched him.

When he had ticked them he said, 'Excellent!'

Dylan said, 'I'll write excellent at the bottom.'

He wrote 'e s l t' and drew a smiley face.

I said, 'I've never seen a sum with three numbers in like those.' (I pointed to the last two sums). 'Did you just make them up?'

George said, 'No, (he got a dice) it's like when you throw the dice then get a + 5 then a + 1 and then (turns dice over to − 4) and − 4 like that.'

Dylan said, 'I just knew it after George said it. We know what each other's thinking and doing.'

Here again a fabulous example of sustained shared thinking.

Revisiting the definition of sustained shared thinking, it seemed that more and more of my observations fulfilled the criteria.

> An episode in which two or more individuals work together in an intellectual way to solve a problem, clarify a concept, evaluate activities, extend a narrative, etc. Both parties must contribute to the thinking and it must develop and extend.'
>
> (Siraj-Blatchford et al 2002:8)

I noticed that the frequency as well as the duration of these episodes had increased dramatically since the start of the project. The children have developed a positive attitude towards maths and solving problems. They talk confidently about how they work things out and what they have learned. They are able to make connections and extend their learning through sustained shared thinking. The children's ability to think and learn, and then effectively communicate their findings, certainly kept surprising me.

When Katy and George produced their books during the last week of the project, which had lasted for only four and a half months, they were my last pieces of evidence collected. Katy and George wanted me to photocopy the books so they could put them on the maths shelves for their friends to complete. Again we were all surprised. Their inventiveness, confidence, perseverance and self-motivation seemed to have no limits.

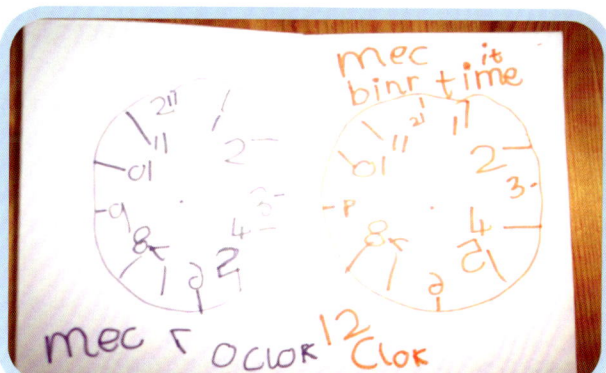

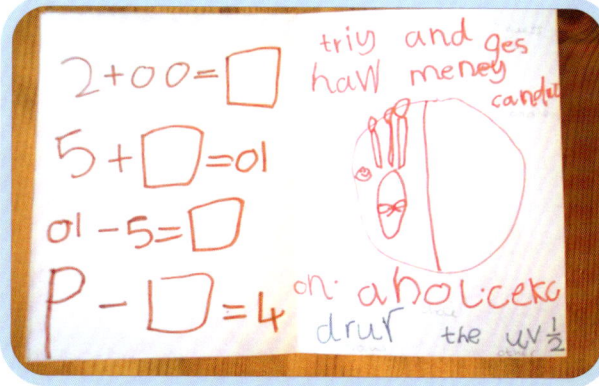

Many of the children enjoyed filling in the books and of course they then made some books of their own!

Dylan's learning story.

Perhaps one of the most interesting themes weaving through the months of research was Dylan's learning story. Dylan is an outgoing, confident child with a wide general knowledge that he eloquently shares with us all, but I learned so much more about him through my observations.

Dylan settled very quickly into Class 1 and thoroughly enjoyed school. Our play-based curriculum was well suited to his needs and he sailed through his first term at school. He learned to recognise some numbers and letters during adult-led activities. He enjoyed the varied activities we provided during these sessions, looking, listening, talking, moving, singing, sharing, handling real objects and materials.

Just before this project started, we noticed a change in Dylan. He was not so keen to participate in group activities. He had noticed that his close friends could do more than him during these sessions and his self-esteem plummeted.

I was aware of the work of Daniel Goleman (1995) on emotional intelligence and reread some of his work.

Goleman identifies five aspects of emotional literacy:
- self-awareness
- management of emotions
- self-motivation
- handling relationships
- empathy

Dylan was very able to handle relationships and always showed empathy towards the other children, but as he became more aware of what other children could do, those things that he couldn't, his self-esteem and motivation became almost non-existent. He seemed to be developing a fear of being asked, of being wrong. He stopped participating in group sessions and even began to ask for a bucket, saying he felt sick. He didn't seem to be aware that nearly all the children were at the same stage of development as he was.

We all worked hard to help him invent strategies to cope with his fears and anxieties: how to show us when he wanted to be asked a question, how to use the resources in the room to help him, and little tricks to help him remember certain numbers and letters. His friends quickly gave answers for him if he needed them to, and helped him whenever they could.

When I started the research project, I talked to these four children and their parents about the exciting work we were going to do together. This became the turning point for Dylan. The others in the group were his friends, the children he thought could do more than him, children he wanted to be like. They did recognise more numbers and were able to write more carefully, but Dylan soon came to realise that he usually led the group, that they listened to what he said, valued his contributions and appreciated the games he devised.

Within a few weeks of the start of the project, Dylan had got his self-esteem back. He had recovered his 'can do' attitude in maths. Throughout the project Dylan came up with the most amazing strategies when he thought he couldn't do something. For example, in the second game, when he saw Owen writing numbers to 100 in tens he panicked, thought quickly, then announced he was jumbling his numbers up to make it more fun for the animals! Yet, in the same game, he was the one who worked out that throwing two sixes was more than the squares on the board and devised a separate way to record this. Not a child who can't recognise the number 7, but a powerful thinker!

Dylan's powerful mind at work: some observations.

In our fourth session I had invented a game that started in the middle of the board. A few months later Dylan devised his own game that started in the middle. I asked him how he knew where to put the starting line.

I said, 'How did you know that was the middle of the board?'

Dylan replied, 'It's there (pointing to the line) that's the middle. Look, 1, 2, 3, 4, 5 then 1, 2, 3, 4, 5.'

I said, 'Did you just know that or did you work it out?'

'I worked it out. 10, look, 10 squares 1, 2, 3, 4, 5, 6, 7, 8, 9, 10. Then think of 'doublers' and then that's double 5, then that's where it is.'

At this time Dylan still couldn't always recognise the numbers 7, 8 or 9, but he had begun to use number lines and notices from around the room to help him remember.

Later that month when Dylan was working independently, he recorded some 'doublers'.

**We have practically and verbally worked on 'doublers' but never recorded them like this. Dylan often uses 'doublers' in his games - and when he is working inside and out.
He wrote 'buBlr' (doubler) at the top.**

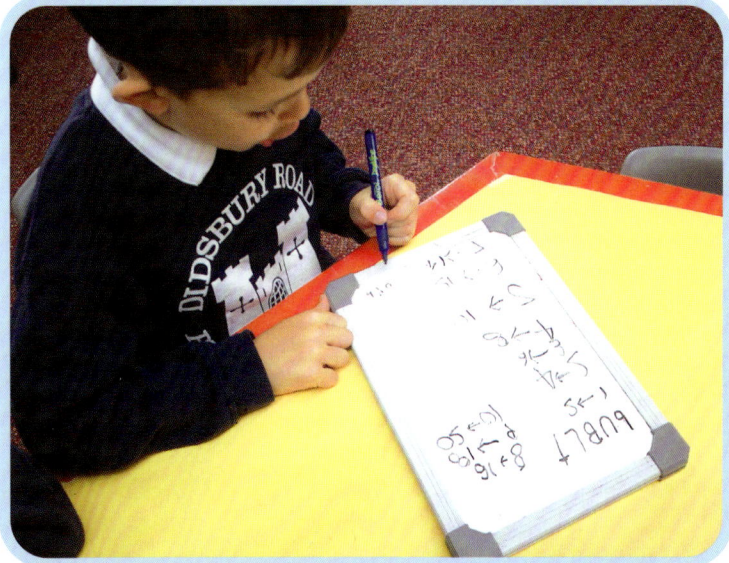

Dylan wrote his first 'doubler' and then worked quickly down to double 7.

We had been talking about putting the largest number in our head (touching the side of our head as we said it) and counting on from there. He did this and counted on the 7 on his fingers. He did the same for 8. He studied the numbers in the first and second columns and smiled and quickly wrote 9 ➜ 18   10 ➜ 20.

When questioned he said, 'I noticed that when I counted 'doubler' 7 it was 2 more and then 8 was 2 more. So I said 2, 4, 6, 8, 10, 12, 14, 16. Then I knew it was 18. It's counting in twos and I know 'doubler' 10 is 20 anyway.'

Dylan showed the class and explained his pattern.

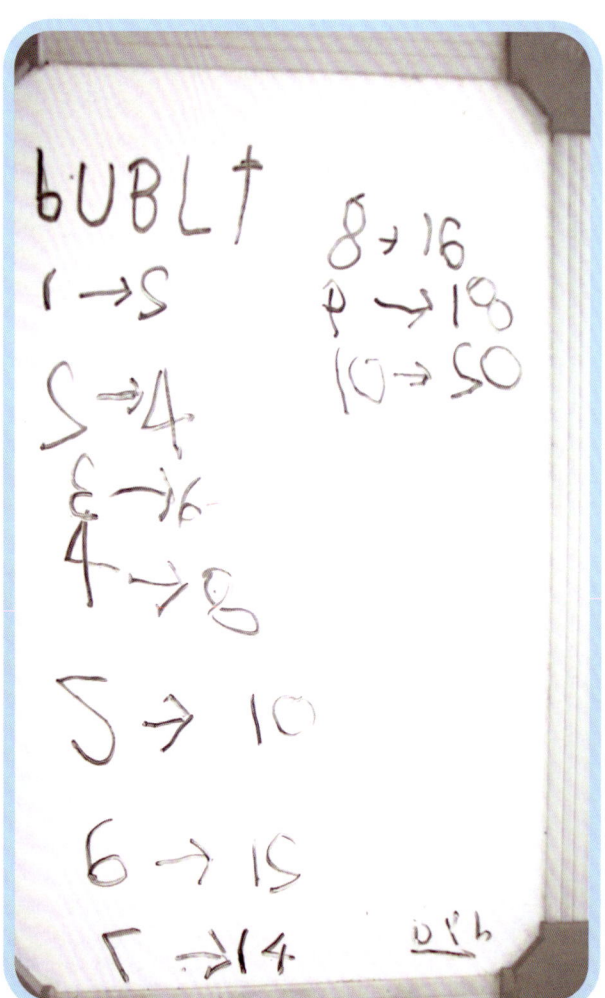

But my notes are full of many more examples of the amazing things Dylan said:

- Asking if I had mixed snowflakes and stars in the boxes to move forward and backwards in games, and explaining how to work out the move correctly.

- Asking to use two dice when I was introducing plus and minus dice and explaining how to work out the sum the two dice made.

- When George had finished in Homer's game and said he would go off the table if he had another go, Dylan immediately said, 'Not if you get take aways.'

- When Dylan said, 'It's good to win but it's all in the heart of the game, playing is most important.'

- 'I know what 100+100 is, it's 200. It's just the same as small numbers. You shouldn't be afraid by numbers, like 500+500 is 1000. It's just the same as ordinary numbers, in small numbers it's 5+5 is 10.'

- His knowledge of whales and the interest it gave to everyone in the game. Dylan said if we drank sea water we would probably die. 'Is it poisonous?' asked Owen. 'No, it's the germs and chemicals that are in it that make it poisonous,' Dylan replied.

- When we were talking about our brain and how we learn, looking, listening, thinking, Dylan said, 'If you don't speak out what you know, you're hiding you're a genius.'

- Dylan showing me his way to work out two plus and minus dice by explaining, 'If you get different ones, you take away that from that. If you get two the same, you put them together and then go forwards for adds and backwards for take aways.' He said I'd be impressed, and I was!

... to name just a few!

Dylan enjoys maths and the challenge of a new game. 'This is easy for me,' he says as he rushes to correct the sequence of numbers in one of Owen's games.

After each game, I always asked the children what they had learned in that game. Nearing the end of the project I asked the children separately what they had learned about games and about maths.

On this occasion I used an interview technique that we had acted out as part of our class assembly, when Dylan had been the 'host' in our Super Sonic Science Show. He had used a microphone and asked lots of questions.

I used the same line he had used in his interview, although he was much more flamboyant than me! I said, 'Dylan Serventi, can you tell me what you know about... playing games. Tell me what you've learnt as well!'

On the following two pages you can read some of Dylan's thoughts. He had learned so much.

Games are good for helping you learn. In our games I learnt numbers and adding, take aways, not cheating (laughs!) In the snow game I did 3D shapes and cubes and cylinders and cones that stick up Homer's bum. Remember that one Ms Hill? Then I nearly remembered the 7 and 8 and 9 didn't I? But sometimes I don't, do I?

My 'Race against Time' is a good game, well George and Dylan's actually. I had to listen and talk to George. I wanted to play teams but George didn't, so we talked about it and we had to decide and we decided not to. Then we had to plan what to do and then we drew it and then made the rules. Then at the end we had to play it to see if it worked right. It did.

I love playing these games 'coz we get to invent them. A good game is if it's like a play. Teachers don't need to make them up. We've made the rules and made the game and we are the inventers of games. We are the best at inventing games you've ever seen, aren't we?

What have you learned about
GAMES?

The best game was the take away and adds. That started in the middle and me and George were brothers and we both got eaten by the shark and our Mums cried. The Mums were the winners in that game, well Katy and Owen's, ours were unlucky. Unlucky for some!

It doesn't seem like you're learning when you play games: you get into it and do learn.
We do learn, don't we? You always ask us what we learnt, didn't you and then we tell you. So then we must have learnt lots of things.

- The one who rolls the highest number starts first.

- You go clockwise this way or anticlockwise that way.

- You have to listen to others.

- Share with your friends.

- Take turns and help them.

- Don't cheat, which I need to remember don't I!

- If you cheat, you need to take the first throw you get and not waste valuable time.

- You can play yourself. You can be a mover.

Numbers are for saying and counting and adding and taking away and you can move forward in games for add and back for takeaways. When you use two dice you add them together like 4 add 4 is 8. That's a sum that is: 4 + 4 makes 8 - it's a double too. Doubles are two numbers the same and when you add them together you say... that's double, two lots of the same number. Double 2 is 4, double 3 is 6, double 4... oh I did that, double 5 is 10. Me and George call them 'doublers'. 'Doublers' are easy for me.

I don't always know 7, 8 or 9 do I? Even though sometimes I do, I can count past them but its just remembering those numbers 7 8 9 ! I know 99 and 100 and they are much bigger numbers. You don't have to be scared of numbers, not even big numbers. Numbers can be worked out by your own brain and it's very important to have numbers, isn't it?

The one with the highest number on the red dice starts the game. If you get a 6 it is the biggest on the dice so no one can beat you, but if someone gets a 6 just you two have to throw to see who gets the most out of you two. It doesn't matter what the others get. Two getting 6s is like 'doublers' isn't it?

What have you learned about
MATHS?

I know all about shapes and then we played the Homer game. There are flat shapes and there are 2D shapes and when you stick them together they make 3 dimension shapes like Homer's. Like circles the same size all stuck together make a cylinder. We did that with the 'cheddars' didn't we? It was a cylinder and we opened it and there was lots of flat circles inside. I had two 'cheddars', yum yum. The sphere was an orange wasn't it? It was circles of different sizes, starting with a small one and getting bigger and bigger and then going back to small ones. If you don't put them together in the right order it will make a 3D shape called Spherasourus.
It will look like the back of a dinosaur. 'Do you know any more shapes?' Yeah, lots, squares and oblongs and triangles and diamonds and stars and cubes and those boids, what are they called? 'Cuboids.' Yes, cuboids.

- If they didn't have numbers in the world it would be hard for everyone. No one would know how much it is in the shop and how many they want to buy.

- When you have clocks they have numbers on and then you can tell the time. The big pointer goes around the circle this way, clockwise, and when it gets back to 12 the other one moves to the next number 1 then it's all the way round and it moves to 2. That's the way to tell the time.

- When you need to add numbers you can use fingers or counters, like the snowflakes and stars, but sometimes you just know what it is, like the 'doublers' (laughs) and when you add zero. (laughs)

How do you work out 7, 8 and 9 so you can say and write them?
Well everyone has a computer in their brain and they use it to help them remember things and store information. I need it especially for remembering 7, 8 and 9. If I see those numbers, my computer starts up and pings. Then a line of numbers come on the screen, 1, 2, 3, 4, 5, 6, 7, 8, 9, 10 then I look at the 10 and go backwards. If I see that (points to 8) I see the numbers on my computer and the pointer goes to the 10 and I say (whispers) 10, 9 and then (says loudly) 8. I don't do that for the other numbers. I know them already. 'What about 88?' I just know that. What number is on your front door? (thinks, then says) 9. How did you remember that? My computer told me (points to head).

When I had finished writing about the gamesters, I gave Dylan's mother and father the report to read. Although we'd had many discussions about Dylan during his year in Class 1, I wanted to ensure they were happy with what I was writing. I also wanted to include some of their thoughts and feelings.

This is what they wrote.

Before the project

At the end of Dylan's very first day in school at bed time, he said, 'I'm useless Mum'. When asked 'Why?' he said, 'Because I can't read and write.' Over the first term in school, Dylan became progressively anxious and reluctant to attend, particularly if he thought he was going to be asked to write. On these days he woke very early and immediately began to express deep anxiety and concern about the day ahead in relation to being asked to do written work. He often complained of 'feeling sick' and asked if he could have the day off. Up until this point we had always known Dylan was intellectually very able but we had also seen him as an emotionally resilient child. This anxiety, distress and reluctance to go to school came as an incredible shock. We were both obviously really upset and struggled to support him.

During the project...and after

Dylan's teachers were fantastically empathetic and went out of their way to boost his confidence and encourage him to cope. We were delighted when Ms Hill described the Early Excellence work and asked if Dylan could be included in her group. This input had a powerfully positive impact on Dylan's emotional well-being and as a consequence we all benefitted as a family.

Within a few weeks Dylan was sleeping in late and we had to wake him up to get him ready for school. He was back to himself, he was keen to get to school and he was happy, socially having great fun. Reports of anxiety and distress in school petered out. He was physically much healthier too, following a term of flu and sickness when he was at his most distressed.

Dylan is creative, perceptive, very keen to learn. He has great general knowledge and is a superb problem solver. The Gamesters approach to learning enabled him to demonstrate these strengths and did not focus much on his literacy weakness. This approach enabled him to feel good about himself again, to demonstrate on a regular and intensive basis both to his teacher and peers what a clever boy he is. He could experience feeling equal to his classmates, because in this setting, he is.

Dylan loves working in a team, he is not a competitive learner. With this approach he felt relaxed and was able to access his creativity and imagination. He loved working with his friend George and they talked about what they had created outside of the sessions. They laughed loads!

We appreciate how lucky Dylan is to have been included in this group. Ms Hill has made some fantastic and detailed observations of him and given us a wonderful record of his comments. His humour is evident throughout her work with him, which was great for us to read. This intense time she had with Dylan has bonded him to her (and us to her!). He has continued this year to seek Ms Hill out when he has felt 'wobbly'. He feels she knows and understands him.

Yes, Dylan did benefit from being part of the project, but of course the benefits were mutual. I know I learned so much from Dylan and Katy, George and Owen, as did the staff and all the other children in Class 1.

'Start at the beginning and keep going till you get to the end, then you're a winner!' said Owen.

As I look back at the evidence I collected, I know we are all winners.

Everyone including the group of four children, the whole of Class 1 and all the adults working in our reception classes are winners. I feel particularly privileged to have been involved in the project with Katy, Dylan, Owen and George. I had thought to write 'leading' the project, but I feel the children did that admirably for themselves!

I can imagine how Vivian Gussin Paley felt when she wrote these powerful sentences while researching with young children. I know it sums up how I felt when I was involved in this project. I read it often, as I know it's how I want to go on feeling every day when I work with children.

> When they said things that surprised me, exposing ideas I did not imagine they held, my excitement mounted and I could feel myself transcribing their words even as they spoke. I kept the children talking, savouring the uniqueness of responses so singularly different from mine. The rules of teaching had changed: I now wanted to hear the answers I could not myself invent.   (Paley 1986:126)

Children have a natural curiosity; they all want to learn, as these gamesters have so brilliantly proved! Harnessing their natural curiosity, as well as allowing them to share ownership of what was being taught and learned, provided many opportunities for sustained shared thinking.

As I became more involved in the project I started to ask myself questions about sustained shared thinking.

- Does sustained shared thinking just happen?
- Does it happen to everyone?
- Does it happen every day?
- When does it happen?
- Where does it happen?

Thinking about these questions, I began to see more clearly the factors that affected both the opportunities for, and the levels of, sustained shared thinking.

My observations taught me that the quality of children's thinking can rise dramatically when:

- They are offered well-organised and stimulating resources that reflect the children's natural interests.
- They are given time to be playful, in a secure environment, which allows them to take risks and make connections in their learning.
- They are assisted by reflective and questioning adults and, of course, by all the other thinking children in the class.

The role of the adult is crucial in children's learning. Planning is essential, but I began to wonder if great plans always mean great learning? Unfortunately not. More questions began to shape themselves in my mind.

Does the planning allow for:

- freedom to explore
- time to experiment
- opportunities to act independently
- time to reflect on their findings
- making connections
- taking learning forward

Is there actually TIME for sustained shared thinking?

Critically examining my planning opened up a whole new world for the children and the adults! BUT even a new approach to planning is not enough. My observations showed that other factors were at work. The quality of children's learning is strongly influenced by the adults' expectations. When their expectations are high, the quality of learning is high. But high expectations can create anxiety and fear of failure. Creating a classroom culture where 'no-one is a loser' makes all the children feel safe. I can raise expectations and demands, sensitively and encouragingly. I can raise their levels of enthusiasm and engagement, as well as their levels of achievement. Everyone can be a winner!

Near the end of the project, Dylan expressed his concern about the group not playing games with me when they moved on to Year 1.

I suggested they could teach their new teacher how to play games, to which Dylan replied, 'Us five all think the same way don't we? We should still do them and in Year 2 and 3, well, 'til we all leave this school.'

I have already purchased a game board for their next teacher!

As Owen said, 'Start at the beginning and keep going 'til you get to the end, then you're a winner!'

We started at the beginning and we certainly kept going, although somehow I don't think this journey will ever have an end.

The winners:
Katy, George, Dylan
and Owen.

Acknowledgements

So many people to thank!

Many thanks to Jenny and Liz, the directors of Early Excellence, for giving me the opportunity to be involved in the project and for their support and encouragement during the long process of writing.
A special thank you to Mary Jane; she inspired me before, during and after this project with the gamesters. Writing this has been a steep learning curve for me and I am extremely grateful for her support.
Thanks to my two children: Sam for his continuous help and patience with my computer skills and Sally for pointing out most of my mistakes before anyone else saw them!
Many thanks to my colleagues, Mrs Furmidge, Mrs Lyons, Mrs Thirsk and Mrs Rathbone for their assistance during the project and supporting me in finishing! Thanks to all the children in Class 1 who also enjoyed and contributed to the project.
Thanks to the parents of the four children involved for their observations, comments, enthusiasm and letting me use their children.

Above all, of course, the biggest thanks to Katy, Dylan, George and Owen for letting me be a gamester too!

References

Drummond, M.J. (1995) *In School at Four: Hampshire's earlier admissions programme* Hampshire: Hampshire County Council Education Department

Goleman, D. (1996) *Emotional Intelligence. Why it Can Matter more than IQ* London: Bloomsbury

Paley, V.G. (1986) *On Listening to What the Children Say* Harvard Educational Review 56.2.122-131

Paley, V.G. (2004) *A Child's Work* Chicago: Chicago University Press

Siraj-Blatchford, I., Sylva, K., Muttock, S., Gilden, R. & Bell, D. (2002) *Researching effective pedagogy in the early years* Research Report RR356 London: DfES

Afterwords

3

Mary Jane Drummond

Lesley Hill's learning story

It has been a privilege to participate, in a minor role, in Lesley Hill's practitioner research project, and to read the successive drafts of her enthralling account of four emergent mathematicians, playing their hearts out in the security of their small group. Like Liz Marsden and Jenny Woodbridge, who introduced Lesley Hill's work in part one, I see the completed report as a journey, a journey around a whole anthology of classroom stories. One story is about the irrepressible Dylan, of course, and another about what Vivian Gussin Paley, the incomparable story teller of kindergarten life, calls 'the kindness of children' (Paley 1999). There's a story about Lesley Hill herself, depicted in the throes (and thrills) of becoming a teacher-researcher; and there's a story about planning and provision, proving, once and for all, that less can mean more. The story about children's play is one of the most powerful, demonstrating quite conclusively the truth of Piaget's great one-liner 'Play is a form of thought' (Piaget 1951:161). Finally, there is a wonderful story about children talking, not just chatting, but thinking aloud, with energy and zest, with piercing insight and unpredictable humour. This last story reads like an extended illustration of Robin Alexander's beautifully argued case for 'dialogic teaching,' in which he insists 'Talk is the true foundation of learning' (Alexander 2004:5). Each of these stories, some of which are explored in more detail below, illustrates one or more aspects of the Early Excellence pedagogical model (presented on p4); taken together, they show how a reflective and enquiring teacher translates principles into practice, and in the process, illuminates what the great educator Susan Isaacs calls the relation between understanding and purpose (1932:70).

The story of Dylan

The penultimate chapter of Lesley Hill's report is a sensitive and admiring account of Dylan's nimble mind at work. My own favourite example of his distinctive cast of mind comes in an earlier chapter, describing the game at which plus and minus dice were introduced for the first time. At the end of the game, Lesley Hill invites the children to review their learning, one by one. George's learning is about addition: 'I've learned that numbers are special to add together to get bigger.' Lesley Hill responds in supportive and didactic mode, rephrasing this comment to establish a basic principle: 'You're right George, if you add two numbers together you get a bigger number, you get more.' Quick as a flash, Dylan sees the chink in this reasoning, and pounces: 'Except of course with zero.' We can almost hear Lesley Hill's gasp of astonishment and admiration.

Dylan's confidence here, his spontaneous insight into numbers and how they work, and his willingness to challenge his teacher, are in striking contrast to the attitude of 'learned helplessness' described elsewhere in this report by both his teacher and his mother. In this extract, we see a young learner who is far from helpless, a learner with all the characteristics that Dweck and other researchers associate with a 'mastery orientation' (Dweck & Leggett 1988, Sylva 1994) (1). Dylan's earlier helplessness, expressed in anxiety and distress, has given way to a proud assumption of being at home in the work, master of all he surveys, making new meanings, new connections, playing with ideas for the sheer joy of it. How else can we explain the Scottish theme of the game entitled 'The Race Against Time and Loch Ness Monsters', especially the little red legs hanging down from the top of the page, explained by Dylan as 'the legs of the man from Scotland'. When asked how he and George might improve this game, George suggests some little shoes 'to make it look real', and Dylan 'a smelly pong for those feet!'

(1) In an ingenious series of experiments involving problem solving, where some tasks ensured success and others failure, Dweck and Leggett found two different patterns of behaviour. 'Mastery' orientated children stayed positively on task, even when they encountered failure; they saw the more difficult problems as interesting challenges to be mastered through effort. But other children responded in a 'helpless' way; they disengaged from the task, started to chat among themselves, and showed signs of negative feelings.

Reading this passage, I was reminded of the argument advanced by Loris Malaguzzi, one of the founding members of the Reggio Emilia approach to early education, that for young children the logic of things and the logic of imagination are not in opposition but in harmony, in a relationship of reciprocity. This relationship, he writes, is in keeping with the desires and nature of children, whose identity emerges by 'bringing together the frontiers of the real world, those of the possible and the impossible' (Malaguzzi, 1996:48).

Great expectations

For all that Katy, George, Owen and Dylan are centre stage throughout this report, there is plenty of action on the teacher's side of the story. As we read, we see a teacher moving out of the comfort zone, slowly, beginning to ask herself difficult questions and learning, all the time: learning to keep quiet, learning to be surprised, learning to respect children's capacity to challenge and stretch themselves, learning a new orientation to planning and provision. Malaguzzi identifies this particular kind of planning as one of the key principles of the Reggio Emilia approach: 'the teachers follow the children not the plans' (Malaguzzi 1993:85).

But we also see a teacher who meets another of Malaguzzi's requirements; describing the Reggio view of children as 'highly optimistic,' since children have 'an extraordinary potential which has never ceased to amaze us,' he goes on to summarise his thoughts, saying, 'This is a gifted child, for whom we need a gifted teacher.' In my view, Lesley Hill is just such a teacher, offering her children the gifts of her attentive listening, of security, of her capacity for self-criticism – and, above all, the gift of time. Since her expectations of children are so high, she is prepared to give them all the time and space they need to exercise their amazing powers of thought, to realise their 'extraordinary potential'. In the safe, slow world of play, in the secure space of the tranquil Friday morning sessions, we see these four children rising to their teacher's expectations, and, indeed, outstripping them.

The genius of play

This wonderful phrase, the title of a wonderful book by Sally Jenkinson (2001), is not too strong to describe the richness and complexity of the play that Lesley Hill has documented. For a long time, I have argued the desirability of thinking of 'play' in its noun form, not as a verb, not as something children do, but as a place and a time in which they exercise their growing powers – of many, many different kinds (Drummond 1996:137-8). In play, I maintain, under a bush or up a tree, alone or in small groups, with blocks, or silver shoes, or penguins and sharks, children do and think and feel and understand in ways of the greatest importance.

So, in the play reported here, we see powerful children, doing important things. Because, in Lesley Hill's own words, 'they were *playing* at maths,' they were deeply engaged, highly motivated, intensely purposeful thinkers. And because the time and spaces for their play were long, capacious, unhurried, the children's thought took many diverse forms. We can see so many different kinds of thinking in action in their play. They think in the present tense, doing running commentaries, making comparisons, evaluations and interpretations. They think ahead, planning, seeing possibilities, speculating, wondering, dreaming. They think back, reviewing, reporting, remembering, re-creating. They think sympathetically, projecting themselves, sensitively, into the thoughts and feelings of others. They think imaginatively, effortlessly spinning stories, characters and plots (just think back to the penguins walking in the snowy park, in the very first game, and Owen and Katy's game where the baby rabbit has to escape from the maze, get to his Mummy and give her a kiss). They think collaboratively, solving problems together: look at Owen and Katy again, working out how to draw the maze 'for rabbits not to be lost in.' They think rationally, explaining, justifying, giving different reasons, making a case, defending

a position. They think morally, exploring their spontaneous sense of justice and injustice, establishing the rules of a harmonious and equitable society. Katy declares the principle 'everyone's a winner in our games'; it's the dawn of a classroom culture where no-one is a loser.

Their play is indeed 'a form of thought', but who would have expected that so much thinking, in so many forms, could have been stimulated by a plain, white, empty game board? Less *does* mean more.

The sum of the parts

Perhaps, after all, the biggest and best story is a transformation story about the big picture; about how the familiar classroom culture, in which Lesley Hill and her colleagues prepared four and five year old children for the challenges of Key Stage One, became a very different place, a place of curiosity, open-mindedness and reflection, where a genuine research enquiry took place. In a provocative discussion of what it is to be a teacher-researcher, Glenda Bissex, herself an adventurous teacher and researcher, explains that a teacher-researcher is

'an observer

　　　　a questioner

　　　　　　　a learner

　　　　　　　　　and a more complete teacher.'

(Bissex and Bullock 1987)

More complete, Bissex argues, because the artificial distinction between knowing and doing that is characteristic of our education system has been broken down. The teachers who *do,* 'who are not trusted, and often do not trust themselves, to know what and how they should teach,' have become teachers who also *know,* because they have done the research; they no longer have to choose between knowing and doing.

Furthermore, it seems to me, the classroom of a teacher-researcher becomes more complete. More complete because more focussed attention is paid to every element of the Early Excellence pedagogical model, more attention is given to the relationships between the elements, and more importance is attached to the culture in which the whole is embedded. Many years ago, the inspiring and influential Lawrence Stenhouse, a pioneer of the whole teacher-as-researcher movement, wrote that 'a good classroom is one in which things are learned every day which the *teacher* did not previously know' (my emphasis) (Stenhouse 1975:37). And, we may add, in this good classroom, where teachers learn just as much as their children do, where teachers ask questions of themselves as well as of their children, there are emotional benefits too. In the safety of this good classroom, where the ethos is governed by the marvellous Montessori principle of 'trust in the safety of freedom' (Fisher 1913:125), we may conclude, as Lesley Hill does, 'no-one is a loser...everyone can be a winner.'

Early Excellence – the big picture

In the final pages of this book I reflect on what I see as the significance of the Early Excellence pedagogical model. I have been working closely with Early Excellence since early 2003, and more intensively since the spring of 2004, when the practitioner research programme was launched. It was a great privilege for me to work with 15 talented and committed early years educators over the next nine months and to support them in their fascinating classroom enquiries. This protracted working relationship has helped me to see more clearly what it is that Early Excellence has to contribute to the growing professionalism of the early years community, through their training programmes, their resource centre and, especially, through their pedagogical model, here published for the first time. In part one, Liz Marsden and Jenny Woodbridge introduced their model and explained what they see as the critical factors in effective learning and teaching. To complement their introduction I have identified three distinctive features of the model that seem to me to be worthy of further elaboration.

The need for roots

One of my most treasured possessions is a stained, battered and dog-eared photocopy of a set of discussion papers prepared by Margaret Carr and her colleagues at the University of Waikato, New Zealand during the years of intensive work that preceded the publication of the enormously influential bilingual curriculum document *Te Whāriki* (in draft form, for consultation in 1993 and in its final, official, approved form in 1996). When the draft document arrived in England, it was the stimulus for a period of sustained shared thinking and writing, instigated and co-ordinated by the Early Childhood Education Forum (ECEF), which led to the publication *Quality in Diversity* (ECEF 1998). Unlike *Te Whāriki, Quality in Diversity* is not a curriculum document, rather a framework for early years practitioners to use in thinking about children's learning; in many other respects it can be seen as the English version of *Te Whāriki*. But the discussion papers that preceded the New Zealand publication are of a very different order. In them, a number of distinguished writers, academics and researchers, set out their best understanding of how to develop a worthwhile curriculum for children from birth to six. They do this through a series of rigorous and far-reaching reviews of the literature on every aspect of early childhood.

The consequence of these far-reaching studies is that every line of the document that followed, *Te Whāriki* itself, is based on empirical evidence and on the hard-won insights of our honoured predecessors in the vast field of early education. Every proposition in *Te Whāriki,* every smallest strand of its all-encompassing framework, is rooted in the shared professional knowledge of its authors; the discussion papers document the sources of their comprehensive understanding.

The Early Excellence model was designed to serve a very different purpose from the New Zealand Ministry of Education document. But it does share this important characteristic: that every element of it can be traced to its roots in the work of other writers and researchers, to the great pioneers of early years education, in this country and elsewhere, and to contemporary developments in thinking, not least in Reggio Emilia, Italy and, indeed, New Zealand.

The emphasis on children's emotional well-being, for example, one of the core ideas outlined on p3, echoes one of the strands of the *Te Whāriki* document, to be sure; but for an English reader its roots stretch further back, and can be found in the writings of Susan Isaacs, whose work at the experimental Malting House school in the 1920s, and subsequent teaching at the London Institute of Education until her death in 1948, are still of enormous importance for early years practitioners today. One of the

keynotes of her thought is the essential interconnectedness of young children's intellectual and emotional development, the impossibility of separating affect from cognition. She writes, for example, 'The thirst for understanding springs from the child's deepest emotional needs; (it is) a veritable passion' (1932:113). This powerful insight is constantly emphasised by Dorothy Gardner, her only English biographer: 'no-one who studied with her' (as Gardner had done) 'would be tempted to forget that children cannot be really emotionally satisfied unless they can also learn, nor really learn unless their emotional needs are met' (Gardner 1969:149).

There are further strong connections with Isaacs' work in the Early Excellence emphasis on children's spontaneous activity, their desires and interests (p6). Isaacs' version of these interests and activities, written in 1932, is a vivid definition of children's spontaneity:

- the love of movement and perfecting bodily skills
- the interest in actual things and events, the discovery of the world without
- the delight in make-believe and the expression of the world within.

And of children's desires, a powerful theme in the Early Excellence model, Isaacs writes that only in the infant school, 'before children have been taught to separate learning from playing and knowledge from life, will you see the strength and spontaneity of the wish to know and understand' (1932:113).

It is tempting to multiply examples of parallels between the Early Excellence model and the work of Susan Isaacs, which was itself empirically grounded in her own detailed observations and works of documentation; let us note just one more connection before we move on. In her first major work (1930), in describing the extraordinary resources of the Malting House school and garden, Isaacs uses the unforgettable phrase 'a generous environment'. What more inspiring criterion could there be with which to evaluate the environment we provide for young children, which, is, significantly, one of the three central constructs of the Early Excellence model.

In the second layer of the model, the emphasis shifts to relationships, especially the interaction between children and adults... 'which is the voice of teaching and learning' (p5). The roots of this enormously important concept go back a very long way indeed, through Gordon Wells, Bruner, Vygotsky and many others, to Socrates himself and the long, challenging dialogues with the youth of Athens that Plato documented for posterity. In our own times the important longitudinal study Researching Effective Pedagogy in the Early Years (REPEY) has identified a particular kind of interaction, 'sustained shared thinking,' as a significant factor in early years settings of the highest quality (Siraj-Blatchford et al 2002). And Robin Alexander's recent work *Towards Dialogic Teaching* (2004) is a valuable compilation of the evidence base for a radical re-appraisal of what classroom talk should sound like, and how we should understand it. He argues for the urgent need to:

> transform classroom talk from the familiar closed question/answer/feedback routine into purposeful and productive dialogue, where questions, answers and feedback progressively build into coherent and expanding chains of enquiry and understanding.   (2004:20)

Enough has been said, I hope, to establish that the constituent parts of the Early Excellence model did not suddenly fall from the sky, so to speak, but can all be traced back to their roots – to educational, psychological and philosophical studies, to both contemporary and historical sources, to research and reflection – and that this rootedness contributes to both the strength and the usefulness of the model.

Studying the iceberg

In a recent small-scale study looking at what was happening 'Inside the Foundation Stage' (Adams *et al* 2004), my colleague Elise Alexander and I began to use the idea of an iceberg, which tradition tells us is nine-tenths hidden beneath the surface of the ocean, to describe what we were doing in the classroom observation phase of the study:

> We wanted to investigate more than the tip of the iceberg, as described in the 'Stepping Stones', and look at the richness and complexity of children's learning, below the surface, as the foundations of all later learning are laid down. (2004:12)

We wanted to see more than children achieving individual, isolated skills, learning initial letter sounds, key words, counting, number recognition, for example, in their literacy and numeracy lessons. We saw all these things, certainly, but what about the rest of the iceberg? What big ideas and life-enhancing concepts were children learning in their literacy and numeracy activities? In literacy, for example, was there evidence of young readers learning to exercise their powers of empathy, understanding and imagination? To help us see below the surface, as it were, we used a variety of analytical frameworks; what we saw is another story (and rather a disappointing one).

Since then, however, my work with the participants in the practitioner research programme, and in particular, my involvement with Lesley Hill in the writing of her research story, suggests to me that the Early Excellence model has the invaluable quality of supporting practitioner-researchers in their desire to see 'below the surface'. The model can help them to look more deeply at taken-for-granted practices and provision, to listen more attentively, to evaluate more critically. By helping educators to focus not just on the three chief actors in the scene – child, adult and environment (which the Reggio educators call the third teacher, it is worth remembering) – but also on the complex relationships between them, and the expression of those relationships in planning, play and interaction, the model encourages more comprehensive observation and deeper understanding.

In other words, the model is more than words on paper, it is a practical tool. What is more, it is a tool that can be used every day, in every kind of setting, for every kind of enquiry, from the small-scale to the magnificent. And its usefulness is in its contribution to a very important project indeed. More important than securing an excellent Ofsted report, more important than pushing up Key Stage 1 SATs scores, more important than working to acquire any number of kitemarks of quality, is the project of understanding what is happening below the surface in effective learning and teaching.

From the parts to the whole

For many years now, early years educators have been on the receiving end of a steady stream, if not a cascade, of publications intended to support their commitment to effective learning and teaching. These publications, all benevolent and aspirational, all compiled by people with the very best intentions, have offered the profession a variety of conceptual structures on which to base their work. Before the early learning goals, the stepping stones and the Foundation Stage Profile, came the desirable learning outcomes and the six areas of learning. Before these, in turn, came the HMI series 'Curriculum Matters 2' and the booklet *The Curriculum from 5-16* (DES 1985), where nine areas of learning were proposed. In the same series we were encouraged to use the constructs of knowledge, concepts, skills and attitudes, and the principles of breadth, balance, relevance, differentiation, progression and continuity.

In my view, all these publications suffer from a common flaw: by breaking down the complex whole that is the enterprise of education into smaller and supposedly more manageable parts, they invite the charge of fragmentation and reductionism. What should and must be big, becomes little. Malaguzzi makes a similar objection to pressures from above; he argues that the narrow constructs of the elementary school damage the effectiveness of schools for young children:

> We are prisoners of a model that ends up as a funnel...the funnel is a detestable object...Its purpose is to narrow down what is big into what is small. This choking device is against nature.   (1993:86)

Malaguzzi is not the only one to argue that this process of reduction and fragmentation is against nature – against the nature of learning, and the nature of children as learners. Charles Desforges calls the process 'dismembering'. In a paper given in 1992, and so relating to the currently prevailing model, he writes: 'This so-called analysis is no more than butchery. A corpus of knowledge representing concepts, skills and attitudes is no more use than a heap of limbs. The question is, how does it work when it is together?' (1992:16)

The crucial question that Desforges articulates here is one that the Early Excellence model does much to help us answer. The model is by no means a heap of dead, dismembered limbs; its parts are united within a representation of the whole, where every element works together, in what Liz Marsden and Jenny Woodbridge call 'the culture...that defines the quality of our practice.'

This emphasis on the all-encompassing circle of culture, the uppermost layer of the model, is an open invitation to educators to consider the whole as well as the parts. Important as the parts may be, taken singly they are a one-way street, leading to superficiality and finally to sterility. Rich resources and an alluring environment, without the adult's thoughtful planning, without the life they are given by children's spontaneous, exploratory, imaginative play, create a toyshop, not a site of effective learning and teaching. Adults and children who co-exist in the toyshop, without an egalitarian exchange of germinating ideas and interests, are strangers, unable to speak together about the things that are most important to them. But in the completed circle of this model we can see the interinanimation of each element of the whole, and, if we look closely enough, even into our own inevitably inadequate practices, we may glimpse the splendid vision of wholly effective learning and teaching in action.

Mary Jane Drummond
Langthwaite May 2005

References

Adams, S., Alexander, A., Drummond, M.J. & Moyles, J. (2004) *Inside the Foundation Stage: recreating the reception year* London: Association of Teachers & Lecturers (ATL)

Alexander, R. (2004) *Towards Dialogic Teaching: Rethinking classroom talk* Dialogos

Bissex, G. & Bullock, R. (eds) (1987) *Seeing for Ourselves – Case Study Research by Teachers of Writing* Portsmouth NH: Heinemann

Department of Education & Science (1985) *The Curriculum from 5-16* London: HMSO

Desforges, C. (1992) *Children's Learning: has it improved?* Paper presented at the ASPE annual conference, Cheshire 1992

Drummond, M.J. (1996) Play, Learning & the National Curriculum: Some Possibilities in Cox, T. (ed) *The National Curriculum and the Early Years* London: Falmer Press

Dweck, C. & Legget, E. (1988) A social-cognitive approach to motivation and personality *Psychological Review* 95 (2) 256-273

Early Childhood Education Forum (1998) *Quality in Diversity in early learning: a framework for early childhood practitioners* London: National Children's Bureau (Revised edition published in 2003)

Fisher, D.C. (1913) *A Montessori Mother* London: Constable

Gardner, D. (1969) *Susan Isaacs* London: Methuen

Isaacs, S. (1930) *Intellectual Growth in Young Children* London: Routledge & Kegan Paul

Isaacs, S. (1932) *The Children We Teach* London: University of London Press

Jenkinson, S. (2001) *The Genius of Play* Stroud: Hawthorn Books

Malaguzzi, L. (1993) in Edwards, C., Gandini, L. & Forman, G. (eds) *The Hundred Languages of Children: The Reggio Emilia Approach to Early Childhood Education* Norwood NJ: Ablex

Malaguzzi, L. (1996) *The Hundred Languages of Children* (catalogue of the exhibit) Reggio Emilia: Reggio Children

Ministry of Education (1996) *Te Whāriki Early Childhood Curriculum* Wellington, NZ: Learning Media

Paley, V.G. (1999) *The Kindness of Children* Cambridge, Mass: Harvard University Press

Piaget, J. (1951) *Play, dreams and imitation in childhood* London: Heinemann

Siraj-Blatchford, I., Sylva, K., Muttock, S., Gilden, R. & Bell, D. (2002) *Researching Effective Pedagogy in the Early Years* Report No. RR356 London: DfES

Stenhouse, L. (1975) *An Introduction to Curriculum Research and Development* London: Heinemann

Sylva, K. (1994) The Impact of Early Learning on Children's Later Development in Ball, C. Start Right: *The Importance of Early Learning* London Royal Society of Arts